"A wise and unsentimental description of what it is like to be a parent to a child with cerebral palsy—an episodic portrait of a very intimate paternal journey."

—ANDREW SOLOMON, National Book Award–winning author of *Far from the Tree* and *The Noonday Demon*

"*The Fall*, Diogo Mainardi's remarkable celebration of his son Tito, who was born with cerebral palsy because of a doctor's negligence, is intensely moving, rational, literate, and an absolute joy to read from start to finish."

—JOHN BERENDT, *New York Times* best–selling author of *Midnight in the Garden of Good and Evil* and *The City of Falling Angels*

"*The Fall* is a moving portrait of a relationship with a child and a place. It is a rare book: by turns heartbreaking, angry, and lyrical."

—EDMUND DE WAAL, author of *The Hare with Amber Eyes*

"*The Fall* is a memoir from Diogo Mainardi, the great Brazilian journalist/novelist, tracing the life and sufferings of his son Tito. Due to the gross negligence of the hospital in which Tito was born, he has been afflicted with cerebral palsy. Tito's story is told in 424 parts, two or three per page, by turns angry, loving, and poetic, that mirror the number of steps Tito takes between their apartment and that hospital, the greatest number of steps Tito has ever taken without

falling down. Along the way, Diogo ruminates about art history, philosophy, literature, and what it is to love someone unconditionally, through every tribulation that arises, and at whatever cost."

—CONRAD SILVERBERG, Boswell Book Company (Milwaukee, WI)

"Other Press has done it again. What a fabulously intricate and idiosyncratic memoir. And what a gift to readers who, but for this book, could not conceive a parent so ferociously loving—*and continually delighting in*—his disabled child."

—ELIZABETH ALEXANDER, University Book Store (Seattle, WA)

"Much like biblical passages I have attempted to read, I did not know what I was reading when I started *The Fall*. The truth, to borrow Emily Dickinson's turn of phrase, dazzled me gradually. This is a potent prayer from a father to a son, from a father to his new god, this firstborn son with cerebral palsy. It is a gorgeous love letter, comforting and dismaying as any psalm."

—VERONICA BROOKS-SIGLER, Octavia Books (New Orleans, LA)

"I read *The Fall* in a sitting; when I looked up, the world seemed a brighter place. It's a memoir, a secret history, an argument against the accidental, but more than anything, it's an astonishing portrait of a parent's love. This is a tell-everyone-you-know-to-read-it book."

—STEPHEN SPARKS, Green Apple Books (San Francisco, CA)

Diogo Mainardi

the fall

A Father's Memoir
in 424 Steps

TRANSLATED FROM THE PORTUGUESE
BY MARGARET JULL COSTA

OTHER PRESS
NEW YORK

Copyright © Diogo Mainardi 2012
Originally published in Portuguese as *A Queda:
As memórias de um pai em 424 passos* in 2012
by Editora Record, Rio de Janeiro, Brazil.
English translation copyright © Margaret Jull Costa 2014
First published in English in 2014 by Harvill Secker, London.

Production Editor: Yvonne E. Cárdenas
Text Designer: Julie Fry
This book was set in Scala and Scala Sans.

10 9 8 7 6 5 4 3 2 1

Grateful thanks to Faber and Faber for permission to reproduce an excerpt
from Ezra Pound, *ABC of Reading*, copyright © 1934 Ezra Pound, and to
New Directions, acting as agent, for permission to reproduce an excerpt from
a letter written by Ezra Pound to Lina Caico, held in the Lina Caico Papers,
Yale Collection of American Literature, Beinecke Rare Book and Manuscript
Library, copyright © 2013 by Mary de Rachewiltz and Omar S. Pound.

Library of Congress Cataloging-in-Publication Data
Mainardi, Diogo, 1962–
 [Queda. English]
 The fall : a father's memoir in 424 steps / by Diogo Mainardi ; translated
from the Portuguese by Margaret Jull Costa.
 pages cm
 "Originally published in Portuguese as: A Queda: As memórias de um pai
em 424 passos in 2012 by Editora Record, Rio de Janeiro, Brazil."
 ISBN 978-1-59051-700-0 (hardback) — ISBN 978-1-59051-701-7
 1. Tito, 2000— Health. 2. Mainardi, Diogo, 1962– 3. Paralysis, Spastic, in
children — Biography. 4. Fathers and sons — Biography. I. Costa, Margaret
Jull, translator, II. Title.
 RJ496.S6M3514 2014
 616.8′420092—dc23
 [B]

 2014005571

the fall

1

Tito has cerebral palsy.

2

I blame Tito's cerebral palsy on Pietro Lombardo.

In 1489, Pietro Lombardo designed the Scuola Grande di San Marco. And it was the Scuola Grande di San Marco designed by Pietro Lombardo that brought about Tito's cerebral palsy.

3

On 30 September 2000, my wife and I set off for Venice Hospital in Campo Santi Giovanni e Paolo. Our son would be born that day. My wife's name: Anna. Our son's name: yes, that's right, Tito.

When we reached Campo Santi Giovanni e Paolo, next to the statue of Bartolomeo Colleoni, Anna said: "I'm really worried about the birth."

She had expressed the same fear in previous weeks, because Venice Hospital, now looming before us, was known for its medical errors.

I studied its façade for a moment.

Venice Hospital moved into the Scuola Grande di San Marco in 1808. The façade, designed by Pietro Lombardo in 1489, became the hospital's main entrance.

I said: "With a façade like that, I could even accept having a deformed child."

4

Venice Hospital made a mistake during Tito's birth. That mistake brought about his cerebral palsy.

5

Ezra Pound, *ABC of Reading*:

> *A few bits of ornament applied by Pietro Lombardo*
> *...are worth far more than all the sculpture and*
> *"sculptural creation" produced in Italy between*
> *1600 and 1950.*

I went further than Ezra Pound. What I said to my wife, as I contemplated the façade of the Scuola Grande di San Marco, can only be interpreted thus: "Pietro Lombardo is worth far more than my son's cerebral palsy."

In the previous image: *Campo Santi Giovanni e Paolo.*

The painting is by Antonio Canal—or Canaletto. It dates from 1725.

Anna and I, clinging to each other like Siamese twins, are standing by the statue of Bartolomeo Colleoni, on our way to the Scuola Grande di San Marco, the entrance to Venice Hospital, where Tito will be born.

8

How did I end up in a painting by Canaletto?

I was always there. And always will be there. The Canaletto painting is my personal nativity. It captures the moment when my destiny was revealed. Ever since Tito's birth, on 30 September 2000, I have become a miniature man, without face or identity, just as I am in Canaletto's painting. What marks me out is fatherhood. I am merely a man eternally accompanying his wife to the birth of their son.

I am Tito's father. I exist only because Tito exists.

9

As well as praising Pietro Lombardo in *ABC of Reading*, Ezra Pound also praised him in *The Cantos*.

In particular, in Canto XLV, entitled "With *Usura*." Lines 27–28:

…Pietro Lombardo
Came not by usura…

10

Usury, according to Ezra Pound, was a "sin against nature." It had the power to corrupt humanity, preventing art from flourishing.

In Canto XLV, Pietro Lombardo symbolizes the idea of artistic beauty. Evil, represented by usury, is incapable of creating Good, represented by the architecture of Pietro Lombardo.

Looking at the Scuola Grande di San Marco before Tito's birth, I was in the grip of the same stupid aestheticism as Ezra Pound.

Venice Hospital was known for its medical mistakes. Instead of going to a safer hospital, in Mestre or in Padua, I merely made a joke about the possibility of having a deformed child.

I could only associate the perfect art of Pietro Lombardo with an equally perfect birth. Because Good, represented by the architecture of Pietro Lombardo, would be incapable of creating Evil, represented by a bungled birth.

11

Ezra Pound, Canto XLV, line 42:

Usura slayeth the child in the womb

The person who nearly slew Tito in the womb by asphyxiation was the hero of those lines by Ezra Pound, Pietro Lombardo.

From Ezra Pound to Xbox.

The hero of the game *Assassin's Creed II*, Desmond Miles, goes back in time and takes on the identity of an Italian nobleman from the late fifteenth century, Ezio Auditore da Firenze, who scours Venice in order to eliminate the murderers who asphyxiated his father. One of the places he has to pass is the Scuola Grande di San Marco.

I am the Desmond Miles of cerebral palsy. I return to the Venice of the late fifteenth century and, like Ezio Auditore da Firenze, I scour the Scuola Grande di San Marco in search of clues that will lead me to the murderers who asphyxiated Tito.

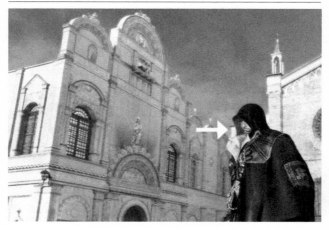

In the previous image: Ezio Auditore da Firenze outside the Scuola Grande di San Marco, poised and ready to destroy his enemies.

The clues that allow you to continue the game (press button Y to get Eagle Vision) can be found behind the upper arch.

John Ruskin, *The Stones of Venice*:

> *The two most refined buildings in this style in Venice are, the small Church of the Miracoli, and the Scuola di San Marco.*

The Scuola Grande di San Marco—as I have said—was designed by Pietro Lombardo. The Church of the Miracoli—I say now—was also designed by him.

If I blame Pietro Lombardo for Tito's cerebral palsy, I should lay equal blame at the door of John Ruskin, who handed me all the necessary clues for interpreting the architecture of Pietro Lombardo. Standing contemplating the Scuola Grande di San Marco, just moments before entering the hospital in Venice, I could see only what John Ruskin had seen before me.

What John Ruskin, with his Eagle Vision, saw before I
ever did:

> *The method of inlaying marble, and the general forms
> of shaft and arch, were adopted from the buildings
> of the twelfth century.*

The Scuola Grande di San Marco, which harked back
nostalgically to the twelfth century, fitted in with what
John Ruskin, in *The Stones of Venice*, called the Byzan-
tine Renaissance.

For John Ruskin, as for me, the best thing about
Pietro Lombardo was precisely that regressive tendency.
For John Ruskin, as for me, the best thing about Pietro
Lombardo was his contrarian reactionaryism.

In 1853, John Ruskin published the third and final vol-
ume of *The Stones of Venice*, entitled *The Fall*.

The architecture of a place, according to him, had
the power to shape the destiny of its inhabitants. The
Byzantine architecture of the twelfth century and the
Gothic Byzantine architecture of the thirteenth, four-
teenth and fifteenth centuries had determined the intel-
lectual and moral superiority of the Venetians, ensuring
their commercial and military hegemony. On the other
hand, Renaissance architecture, which drove out Gothic

Byzantine architecture from the sixteenth century onward, represented an age corrupted by the sense of pride. The same sense of pride that, again according to John Ruskin, finally ruined the city, relegating it to a long period of decline.

Yes: *The Fall.*

John Ruskin pointed out the most harmful elements —or the "immoral elements" that went against the "law of the Spirit"—apparent in the architecture of the Renaissance: Pride of Science, Pride of State and Pride of System.

18

If, as John Ruskin argued, the architecture of a place really does have the power to shape the destiny of its inhabitants, then I could say that the façade of the Scuola Grande di San Marco shaped the birth of Tito.

With its pilasters, its assymetrical arches, its grotesque ornamentation, its colored marble, the Scuola Grande di San Marco harked back to a Byzantine past, untouched by that Renaissance sense of Pride.

To go back to John Ruskin: the architecture of Pietro Lombardo, in the form of the façade of the Scuola Grande di San Marco, exalted the "law of the Spirit," rejecting Pride of Science, Pride of State and Pride of System.

The same could be said of Tito's birth.

Pride of Science? A medical mistake caused his cerebral palsy. Pride of State? Venice Hospital is publicly owned. Pride of System? The system, with its rules, regulations and procedures, failed—failed repeatedly—during Tito's birth.

19

20

In the previous image: Le Corbusier as Ezio Auditore da Firenze, posing outside the Scuola Grande di San Marco, poised to destroy the architecture of Pietro Lombardo.

Yes: *The Fall.*

21

I was born on 22 September 1962.

On that same day, Le Corbusier received an invitation to design a new hospital for Venice, with the hospital being moved from the Scuola Grande di San Marco to the site of the slaughterhouse of San Giobbe.

An event that occurred on the day of my birth could, therefore, have changed Tito's birth.

That's what Tito's story is like: circular.

22

According to Le Corbusier, the streets and squares of Venice resembled the cardiovascular system, with its arteries and ventricles.

The hospital he designed was based on that model, being a kind of great cardiovascular system, comprising a series of terrifying reinforced concrete blocks, joined by a network of ramps and bridges.

Six months after presenting his project, Le Corbusier walked into the sea and died. The reinforced concrete arteries and ventricles of his cardiovascular system stopped working at an opportune moment.

His plan for a new Venice Hospital was buried.

23

Good, represented by the architecture of Pietro Lombardo, generated Evil, represented by a mistake at birth. And Evil, represented by the architecture of Le Corbusier, would have generated Good, because his project for a new Venice Hospital would have been carried out and I would have chosen another place for Tito to be born.

24

Now we live in Rio de Janeiro.

Tito walks on Ipanema beach every day. Today he took two hundred and eighteen steps without falling. Then he fell. He always falls. The sand cushions his fall. He can fall over without grazing his knees or smashing his teeth.

Just like the Scuola Grande di San Marco, Tito's spasticity harks back to the past, paralyzing his motor maturation. I love every Byzantine detail of his motricity.

As with the Scuola Grande di San Marco, Tito is trying to resist the fall. But he always falls. And he always laughs when he falls.

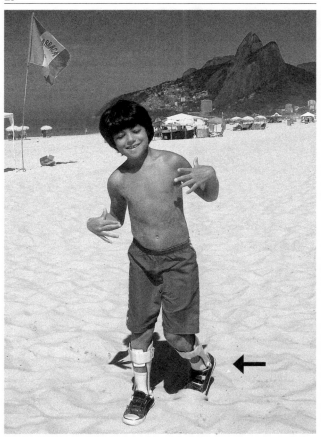

26

In the previous image: one of the two hundred and eighteen steps Tito took on Ipanema beach.

27

My words to Anna, as we stood contemplating the Scuola Grande di San Marco, moments before entering Venice Hospital, came true: "With a façade like that, I could even accept having a deformed child."

I accepted Tito's cerebral palsy.

I accepted it as if it were the most natural thing in the world. I accepted it with delight. I accepted it with enthusiasm. I accepted it with love.

28

On the day Tito was born, Anna and I walked through the gate of the Scuola Grande di San Marco and crossed what used to be the atrium.

29

For more than five hundred years, the Scuola Grande di San Marco was the largest lay confraternity in Venice.

As well as taking in its members when they fell ill or slid into poverty, it also took in the poorest of the city's inhabitants—into that very atrium—guaranteeing them vital support in times of epidemic, scarcity and war.

30

Napoleon Bonaparte occupied Venice in 1797. Some time later, he crowned himself its emperor.

One of his first acts was to suppress the confraternity of the Scuola Grande di San Marco and transform the building into a military hospital.

Napoleon Bonaparte's military hospital, which opened in 1808, was the predecessor of the state hospital where Tito would be born.

31

I blame Pietro Lombardo and John Ruskin for Tito's cerebral palsy.

I also blame Napoleon Bonaparte, without whom the Scuola Grande di San Marco would never have become Venice Hospital.

The Fall of the Bastille resulted in the Fall of *La Serenissima*. The Fall of *La Serenissima* resulted in Tito's many falls.

33

In the previous image: the Fall of the Bastille.

34

The Scuola Grande di San Marco has two floors.

Apart from the porter's lodge to the right, the atrium, on the ground floor, is now deserted.

Anna and I passed through it on our way to the maternity ward.

35

The Sala dell'Albergo on the first floor had paintings by Giovanni Bellini, Paris Bordon and Jacopo Palma il Vecchio.

They were stolen by Napoleon Bonaparte.

The chapter house, next to the Sala dell'Albergo, was adorned with four paintings by Jacopo Tintoretto.

They too were stolen by Napoleon Bonaparte.

36

Nowadays, the first floor of the Scuola Grande di San Marco is occupied by the library of Venice Hospital.

The library contains many rare examples of medical literature from the sixteenth century.

The only one of those books that matters to me is Tommaso Rangone's *How Man Can Live for More than 120 Years.*

37

Tommaso Rangone was the presiding figure at the Scuola Grande di San Marco—its *guardian grande.*

In 1550, he published the medical manual *How Man Can Live for More than 120 Years.*

According to him, in order to reach that age one had to give up a series of foods that were harmful to one's health: lettuce, endive, cabbage, arugula, artichokes, carrots, grapes, figs, melons, eels, milk and cheese. Garlic was injurious to the kidneys and to the ears. Marjoram encouraged fleas. Sturgeon killed babies in the womb.

Tito's sturgeon was the Scuola Grande di San Marco.

38

Before being appointed *guardian grande* of the Scuola Grande di San Marco, Tommaso Rangone was personal astrologer to the commander of the papal guard in Modena.

In 1522, he predicted that in two years' time, in 1524, another Great Flood would occur, because the planets would be lined up under the sign of Pisces, as in the days of Noah. His prediction proved false. Satirical sonnets lampooning him were posted on the city walls. Pietro Aretino called him an "idiot."

Tommaso Rangone changed his identity—he was baptized Tommaso Giannotti—and moved to Venice, where he passed himself off as a doctor, promising to help his patients to live until they were one hundred and twenty.

39

Four and a half centuries before the mistakes made during Tito's birth, therefore, Tommaso Rangone had already linked the name of the Scuola Grande di San Marco with the very worst of medical frauds.

40

How Man Can Live for More than 120 Years was dedicated to Pope Julius III. In his dedication, Tommaso Rangone predicted that the Pope would live a long life. This prediction, as Giacomo Leopardi noted ironically, proved false. Julius III died five years later, at the age of sixty-seven.

41

Giacomo Leopardi alluded to Tommaso Rangone in one of his *Operette morali* (Small Moral Works), entitled "Dialogue Between a Natural Philosopher and a Metaphysician."

> PHYSICIAN: *Eureka! Eureka!*
> METAPHYSICIAN: *What's happened? What is this discovery you've made?*
> PHYSICIAN: *The art of living for a long time…*
> *I will live for all eternity; I will enjoy immortal glory.*

42

By promising to help his patients live until they were one hundred and twenty, Tommaso Rangone amassed a great fortune. He used that great fortune to try to gain eternal life and immortal glory, just like the character in Giacomo Leopardi's dialogue.

Tommaso Rangone discovered—"Eureka! Eureka!" —that the best way of gaining eternal life and immortal glory was to have artists reproduce his image in eternal, immortal works.

He paid for Jacopo Sansovino to adorn the door of the church of San Giuliano or San Zulian with his statue. He paid for Alessandro Vittoria to sculpt his bust for the church of San Geminiano. He paid for Jacopo Tintoretto to feature him in the four paintings commissioned to decorate the chapter house of the Scuola Grande di San Marco.

43

In the first painting, *The Miracle of St. Mark Freeing the Slave*, from 1548, Tintoretto portrayed Tommaso Rangone as a mere witness to the miraculous event, and showed him standing modestly on the left-hand side of the canvas.

In the other paintings, however, commissioned fourteen years later, for eighty ducats each, Jacopo Tintoretto broke all the rules of the age and portrayed Tommaso Rangone as an actual participant in the miracles of St. Mark.

In *St. Mark Saving a Saracen from Shipwreck*, Tommaso Rangone—like a hero from Xbox—goes back in time and is seen on board a boat, vigorously rowing, as he helps the Evangelist save the shipwreck victim from the stormy sea.

In *The Rediscovery of the Body of St. Mark*, Tommaso Rangone goes back in time and is shown kneeling in the cathedral, looking directly up at the saint's soul.

In *The Stealing of St. Mark's Body*, Tommaso Rangone goes back in time to Alexandria, and takes charge of the theft of the martyr's body during a celestial storm.

44

45

In the previous image: *The Stealing of St. Mark's Body*.

The painting is by Jacopo Tintoretto. It dates from 1562.

The arrow indicates the portrait of Tommaso Rangone.

46

In the paintings made by Jacopo Tintoretto for the Scuola Grande di San Marco, Tommaso Rangone was depicted as an aide to the miracle-working saint. This conferred on him the aura of an equally miracle-working doctor.

With his unique talent—and at a cost of eighty ducats per painting—Jacopo Tintoretto eternalized and immortalized medical charlatanism, personified by Tommaso Rangone and made matter in Tito's birth, which took place in the same building four hundred and fifty years later.

An example of Pride of Art?

47

In *The Stealing of St. Mark's Body*, a bearded man stands in the shadows to the right of the picture, next to the camel, watching the scene intently.

It is Jacopo Tintoretto himself.

He depicted himself as a spectator of the theft of the Evangelist's body in exactly the same way in which Alfred Hitchcock appears in *Vertigo*, walking past a shipyard.

48

Vertigo.

When Tito walks, his muscles contract. When his muscles contract, he gets frightened. When he gets frightened, his muscles contract even more.

In Brazil, the title of *Vertigo* was translated as *Um Corpo que Cai*, "A Body Falling." Tito is a body falling.

Each step taken by Tito is the same as a step taken by James Stewart up the bell tower of San Juan Bautista. All right, there's no Alfred Hitchcock. There's no Kim Novak either. There's no Bernard Herrmann soundtrack. But everything else—as I said—is the same. The wide eyes. The open mouth. The dry tongue. The stiff legs. The sweat running down his back. The zoom in. The zoom out.

In the final scenes of *Vertigo*, James Stewart finally overcomes his fear of heights and climbs the bell tower of San Juan Bautista.

He says: "I made it."

Tito, step by step, is making it too.

49

At the end of *Vertigo*, Kim Novak falls from the bell tower of San Juan Bautista. She falls and dies. James Stewart survives. Tito is James Stewart. He falls and survives.

To hell with Kim Novak.

50

51

In the previous image, Tito as James Stewart in *Vertigo*: wobbly, wild-eyed, surrounded by kaleidoscopic spirals, and with a green face.

Tito was green when he was born.

I saw him for the first time in one of the cloisters of Venice Hospital. I had just been talking to the pediatrician who had overseen his birth. He said that Tito had been deprived of oxygen for too long. He also said that Tito would die.

On my way back to the maternity ward, after talking to the pediatrician, I walked past a newborn baby in an incubator. The newborn baby in the incubator had been left in the cloister, parked in a corner. No one was looking after him. Where's the doctor? Where's the nurse? Where's the father?

I glanced at him. I looked again. He wasn't moving, his body was limp and he had a tube up his nose. I read the name written on the label stuck to the lid of the incubator: "Mingardi."

Mingardi was me. I was Mingardi. The newborn baby in the incubator was my son. Mingardi was Mainardi. Venice Hospital even got his name wrong.

I looked at Tito one more time. His face was like mine — except that his was green.

Up until that moment, I had always thought that if my son were to fall into a vegetative state, I would prefer him to die.

After that first contact with Tito in the corridor of the cloister of Venice Hospital, everything changed. All I wanted was for him to survive, because I would always love him and help him in whatever way I could.

Caught between life and death, I clung to life.

54

Lying in the incubator, parked in a cloister in Venice Hospital, Tito, with his green face, was waiting for a boat to take him to the nearest neonatal intensive-care unit, in Padua Hospital.

55

In Padua Hospital, in 1739, George Macaulay graduated as an obstetrician. Some time later, he moved to London and, in 1756, in Brownlow Street Hospital, he became a pioneer in a surgical procedure known as an amniotomy.

A disastrous amniotomy two and a half centuries later sent Tito straight to the intensive-care unit in Padua Hospital.

What came out of Padua Hospital returned to Padua Hospital.

That's what Tito's story is like: circular.

56

The obstetric procedure introduced by George Macaulay consisted of artificially rupturing the amniotic sac in the uterus of the woman giving birth, in order to accelerate labor.

After debating the ethical consequences of the procedure with his colleagues, George Macaulay performed his first amniotomy—on the wife of a haberdasher—using a silver wire.

57

On 30 September 2000, Anna and I crossed the atrium of the Scuola Grande di San Marco, turned to the right, walked through a cloister, went up some stairs and reached the maternity ward of Venice Hospital.

An obstetrician—Dottoressa F—then performed an amniotomy, accelerating Tito's birth.

Apparently without the slightest concern for the ethical consequences of the procedure, she ruptured the amniotic sac in Anna's uterus using an instrument known as an amnihook.

In the previous image: an amnihook.

I blame Tito's cerebral palsy on Pietro Lombardo, John Ruskin, Napoleon Bonaparte and on an amnihook.

Why did Dottoressa F accelerate Tito's birth?

It was never explained to me.

61

The mistakes made by Dottoressa F during Tito's birth were fully documented in the case we brought against Venice Hospital.

An amniotomy is recommended only when the mother is already in active labor and the cervix dilated to at least four centimeters. At the moment when Dottoressa F performed the amniotomy, my wife's cervix was — to use the term in the medical handbook — "impervious."

An amniotomy is recommended only when the fetus's head is in the correct position in the birth canal. At the moment when Dottoressa F performed the amniotomy, Tito's head was certainly not in the correct position, but "very high up (−3cm) and mobile."

62

The amniotomy performed by Dottoressa F was described by experts as "highly inappropriate."

The biggest danger associated with an inappropriate amniotomy is what is called umbilical cord prolapse. That was what happened with Tito. When Dottoressa F ruptured the amniotic sac in Anna's womb, Tito's umbilical cord collapsed, thus cutting off his oxygen supply.

This in turn caused damage to the brain. That brain damage affected his motor apparatus, creating spasticity.

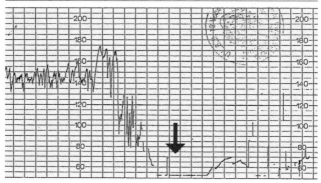

In the previous image: the line of the heart monitor indicates the exact moment when asphyxia caused a dramatic fall in Tito's heart rate.

That was the first of his falls. The original fall.

William John Little was the first to study cerebral palsy.

In 1853, after analysing twenty-four spastic children, he published his lecture series in monograph form under the title *On the Nature & Treatment of the Deformities of the Human Frame,* arguing for the first time that "the spasmodic tetanus-like rigidity and distortion of the limbs of new-born infants [could be] traced to asphyxia neonatorum, and mechanical injury to the foetus immediately before or during parturition."

Some years later, in 1861, at the Obstetrical Society of London, William John Little—basing himself on his analysis of another sixty spastic children—said again that cerebral palsy was the result of birth asphyxia.

To illustrate his thesis, he mentioned the protagonist of Shakespeare's *Richard III*.

According to William John Little, Richard III suffered from cerebral palsy.

Shakespeare described Richard III as "deformed." He also called him "unfinished," "scarce half made up," "cheated of feature," "that bottled spider," "diffused infection of a man," "that foul bunch-backed toad," "bloody dog."

Richard III had "legs of an unequal size." His arm was like "a withered shrub." Nature had made "an envious mountain" of his back. He was "disproportioned in every part."

Shakespeare blamed these deformities on a premature birth.

He tells how Richard III was "sent before [his] time into this breathing world." He also says that "love forswore [him]" in his mother's womb.

At the Obstetrical Society, William John Little, quoting from Shakespeare, said that Richard III's premature birth was secondary to birth asphyxia. And that the asphyxia had caused cerebral palsy.

68

Like Richard III and Tito, William John Little was deformed.

He had contracted polio as a child and this had left him with a club foot. A man with a club foot was the first man to study children with club feet.

69

For Shakespeare, Richard III's deformed body mirrored his deformed character. His cerebral palsy mirrored his evil nature.

In the first acts of *Richard III*, he murders nine people, including his closest relatives and his wife.

In the final act, the ghosts of those nine murdered people return to haunt him in a dream.

70

Tito was my Richard III. Tito was my bunch-backed toad.

He seized my throne. He conquered my kingdom. After his birth, I became a ghost haunting him.

72

In the previous image: Vincent Price in *Tower of London*.

The film was made by Roger Corman in 1962.

Vincent Price played Richard III: deformed, lame, spastic, with a green face.

73

In the case we brought against Venice Hospital, we gave a minute-by-minute account of Tito's birth, based on the data from the heart monitor.

12:35 Normal.

12:40 The needle on the heart monitor suddenly shook. I called the nurse, thinking that this was the first sign of labor. In fact—as I said—this was the first sign of the asphyxia that caused Tito's cerebral palsy. The nurse tried to phone Dottoressa F, but couldn't locate her. She decided to go and look for her. A few minutes later, they returned together.

12:46 Dottoressa F turned off the heart monitor.

12:55 Dottoressa F turned on another heart monitor.
The nurse explained that the previous week one of the machines had failed. During Tito's birth, the first thing to fail was Dottoressa F. As the monitor had correctly shown, Tito was dying.

13:05 Anna was finally taken into the labor ward.

74

Tito was born forty-five minutes after that first fall in his heart rate. According to medico-legal experts, an emergency caesarean like his should have happened less than twenty minutes later.

Another mistake on the part of the hospital.

75

In 1487, in Germany, Inquisitor Heinrich Kramer, a Dominican friar, published his *Malleus maleficarum.*

Chapter XIII of Part II deals specifically with "witch-midwives who commit most Horrid Crimes when they Kill Children." Heinrich Kramer, in *Malleus maleficarum*, recommended that these witch-midwives should be imprisoned and tortured by the religious authorities.

In the last five hundred years, torture has largely fallen into disuse. Despite all the mistakes made during Tito's birth, all I could demand of Venice Hospital was financial compensation.

76

In 1495, eight years after publishing *Malleus maleficarum*, Heinrich Kramer moved to Venice, where he recommended torture as a punishment for witch-midwives who murdered newborn babies.

He stayed at the former Dominican monastery, in Campo Santi Giovanni e Paolo, behind the Scuola Grande di San Marco, which had just been designed by Pietro Lombardo.

In 1808, Napoleon Bonaparte expelled all the monks. The former Dominican monastery was combined with the Scuola Grande di San Marco and converted into a military hospital, which subsequently became a public hospital.

Five centuries later, the same place that had sheltered Heinrich Kramer in 1495 went on to employ Dottoressa F.

That's what Tito's story is like: circular.

77

The cloister in which I saw Tito for the first time, in an incubator, with his face green, belonged to the former Dominican monastery.

On that night, Anna and I slept in one of its rooms.

Tito remained alone in the neonatal intensive-care unit in Padua Hospital, suffering convulsions.

78

The following day, before going to Padua Hospital, I popped into the patisserie Rosa Salva, in Campo Santi Giovanni e Paolo, opposite the Scuola Grande di San Marco.

One of the reasons I had insisted that Tito be born in Venice Hospital, apart from Pietro Lombardo's architecture, was the proximity of the patisserie Rosa Salva.

To go back to Tommaso Rangone: the food that proved most harmful to Tito's health—the one that nearly killed him in the womb—was the *bigné allo spumone di zabaione.*

In the previous image: a *bigné allo spumone di zabaione.*

I blame Tito's cerebral palsy on Pietro Lombardo, John Ruskin, Napoleon Bonaparte, an amnihook, and, lastly, on the *bigné allo spumone di zabaione* made by the patisserie Rosa Salva.

I arrived early at the intensive-care unit in Padua Hospital.

Tito was in an incubator. He lay utterly still. A tube hung from an artery in his foot. Another tube, attached to a ventilator, made one nostril grotesquely large. His body was covered with electrodes connected to a series

of machines. Occasionally, one of those machines gave an alarm signal, and the doctors in the unit would rush over to check what was happening. Whenever they did, I was gripped by the fear that Tito might be dying. That fear filled me with both despair and relief, because I could only be sure that Tito was still alive when I feared that he was dying.

In order to die, Tito had to be alive.

82

I spent the day in the intensive-care unit.

I stroked Tito's face. Still dead. I stroked Tito's chest. Still dead. I stroked Tito's leg. Still dead. I stroked Tito's back. But when I stroked his back, the unexpected happened. He suddenly writhed and arched his spine.

Tito had returned to life.

I cried for half an hour. After crying for half an hour, I cried for another hour. After crying for an hour, I cried for another two hours.

83

The following day, I again visited the intensive-care unit at Padua Hospital.

I immediately stroked Tito's back. He arched his spine even more than he had on the previous day.

I cried for two hours.

When I stopped crying, I remembered the scene in *Abbott and Costello Meet Frankenstein* when the monster,

lying in his tomb, receives an electric shock, violently arches his back and comes to life.

Tito came to life just like Frankenstein's monster.

I cried for another two hours.

84

That night, returning alone on the train to Venice, I realized that each episode of my life corresponded to an Abbott and Costello sketch.

85

Gianni and Pinotto.

That's what the Italians call Abbott and Costello.

They translated *Abbott and Costello Meet Frankenstein* as *Gianni e Pinotto e il cervello di Frankenstein*.

During the week I spent at the intensive-care unit in Padua Hospital, my sole interest was that: *il cervello di Tito*.

Or: Tito's brain.

86

In *Abbott and Costello Meet Frankenstein*, Count Dracula, played by Bela Lugosi, wants to transplant Lou Costello's brain into Frankenstein's monster, played by Glenn Strange.

It worked with Tito.

After his experience in Dottoressa F's laboratory in Venice Hospital, he went on to combine the lack

of motor control of Frankenstein's monster with Lou Costello's buffoonish nature.

87

In Padua Hospital, *il cervello di Tito* was analyzed using ultrasound, electroencephalograms and MRI scans.

No abnormalities were detected.

Up until now, no machine has uncovered the origin of his cerebral palsy.

88

Lou Costello in *Abbott and Costello Meet Frankenstein*: "I've had this brain for thirty years. It hasn't done me any good."

89

90

In the previous image: *Abbott and Costello Meet Franken-stein*.

Glenn Strange is the monster: deformed, ungainly, spastic, green.

91

In 1939, Adolf Hitler received a letter from Richard Kretschmar, a farmhand from Leipzig.

Richard Kretschmar begged Adolf Hitler to help him kill what he, in the letter, called a "monster."

The "monster" was Richard Kretschmar's own son, Gerhard Kretschmar.

Gerhard Kretschmar had been born blind, as well as missing a leg and part of his arm. He had also, accord-ing to his father, been born an "idiot."

92

Adolf Hitler ordered his personal physician, Karl Brandt, to go to Leipzig University and examine Ger-hard Kretschmar for himself.

At the Nuremberg Trials, Karl Brandt gave his own account of events: "If the facts given by the father proved to be true, I was to inform the doctors that, in Hitler's name, they could use euthanasia."

93

After examining Gerhard Kretschmar, Karl Brandt authorized his death.

On 25 July 1939, at the age of five months, Gerhard Kretschmar—blind and with a leg and part of his arm missing and, according to his father, an idiot—was executed with a large dose of the barbiturate Luminal.

94

In a statement made thirty years later, Gerhard Kretschmar's father, Richard Kretschmar, recalled the "euthanasia" of his "monster" in these terms:

> *Karl Brandt explained to me that the Führer was very, very interested in my son's case. The Führer wanted to solve the problem of people who had no future, whose lives were worthless. That is why he had granted a merciful death to our son. Later on, we would be able to have other perfectly healthy children of whom the Reich would be proud.*

An example of Pride of State?

95

Four weeks after the murder of Gerhard Kretschmar, Adolf Hitler's Ministry of the Interior determined that all disabled newborns should be reported to the regime's authorities.

The Ministry of the Interior's rules mentioned in particular those children suffering from "mongolism, microcephaly, hydrocephalus, deformities of the limbs or spine, and paralysis, including spasticity."

That's right: Tito.

96

On 1 September 1939, the Second World War began.

On the same day, Adolf Hitler signed a secret memorandum setting out his euthanasia program.

The memorandum gave doctors the power to "decide whether those who have—as far as can be humanly determined—incurable illnesses can, after the most careful evaluation, be granted a merciful death."

97

Mercy killing. *Gnadentod.*

Euthanasia. *Euthanasie.*

Those were some of the terms used by Nazism to legitimize the mass extermination of disabled newborns.

A worthless life. *Unwertes Leben.*

A life not worth living. *Lebensunwerten Leben.*

Adolf Hitler's "euthanasia" program offered "mercy killings" to those whose lives were "worthless" or "not worth living."

BERLIN, den 1.Sept.1939.

Reichsleiter B o u h l e r und

Dr. med. B r a n d t

sind unter Verantwortung beauftragt, die Befug -

nisse namentlich zu bestimmender Ärzte so zu er -

weitern, dass nach menschlichem Ermessen unheilbar

Kranken bei kritischster Beurteilung ihres Krank -

heitszustandes der Gnadentod gewährt werden kann.

In the previous image: the memorandum signed by Adolf Hitler, granting a mercy killing for Tito.

In the first phase of Adolf Hitler's euthanasia program, five thousand disabled newborns were killed.

The historian Robert Jay Lifton published the testimony of one of the doctors responsible for those deaths, identified simply as Doktor F: "Those who were approved for killing received high doses of Luminal. They were spastic children, incapable of talking or walking. Anyone seeing them would imagine they were sleeping. In fact, they were being killed."

101

After he was born, Tito was taken into the intensive-care unit of Padua Hospital, where he received high doses of Luminal. Anyone seeing him would imagine he was sleeping. In fact, he was being brought back to life.

102

Adolf Hitler's involuntary euthanasia program, known as Action T4, quickly widened its scope. As well as exterminating disabled newborns, it went on, in its second phase, to exterminate disabled adults, the mentally ill, epileptics and alcoholics.

Six hospitals were converted into extermination centers, where the doctors were charged with eliminating patients by injecting them with a mixture of morphine, scopolamine, curare and cyanide.

[46]

104

In the previous image: one of the children suffering from cerebral palsy who was selected to die under the Action T4 program.

105

In the first few months of 1940, in Brandenburg Hospital, Karl Brandt observed an experiment that would change the direction of the Action T4 program.

Twenty patients, confined in a place resembling a public shower room, were gassed to death with carbon monoxide.

Their bodies were immediately cremated by the SS.

106

When Karl Brandt reported back on the result of the Brandenburg experiment, Adolf Hitler decided that all the "biological enemies" of the Third Reich should be eliminated in the same way: gassed and cremated.

107

Biological enemies. *Biologische Feinde.*

Only "racial hygiene" could eliminate the "biological enemies" contaminating the Third Reich.

Racial hygiene. *Rassenhygiene.*

108

In the second quarter of 1940, Adolf Hitler's Ministry of the Interior ordered that an inventory should be made of all Jews in the Action T4 program.

In June of that year, the first group of two hundred Jews, from a psychiatric hospital in Berlin, were gassed and cremated at Brandenburg Hospital.

109

The extermination of Gerhard Kretschmar—a disabled child rejected by his father—had become the extermination of a whole people: the Holocaust.

110

In less than two years, Action T4 killed more than a hundred thousand people.

Adolf Hitler stopped the program on 24 August 1941.

Two months later, the first large extermination camp, under the command of the SS, was opened near Chelmno, and there all the biological and ideological enemies of Germany, the disabled and the Jews, were gassed and cremated on an industrial scale.

In the following months, extermination camps were opened at Belzec, Sobibor, Majdanek, Treblinka and Auschwitz.

111

The administrator of Action T4, Franz Stangl, who was responsible for the deaths of thirty thousand disabled people at the euthanasia center of Schloss Hartheim, became the first commandant of the Sobibor extermination camp.

Between May and August 1942, he killed a hundred thousand Jews.

Franz Stangl was promoted to the post of commandant at the extermination camp Treblinka II.

Between August 1942 and August 1943, he killed another eight hundred thousand Jews.

112

After the fall of the Third Reich, Franz Stangl fled to Brazil.

Pursued by Simon Wiesenthal, he was arrested on 28 February 1967 and extradited to Germany.

Found guilty of the deaths of more than nine hundred thousand people—among them the cerebral palsy sufferers from Action T4 and the Jews from Operation Reinhard—he died in his cell in Düsseldorf.

113

Like Franz Stangl, Josef Mengele also fled to Brazil.

As an SS doctor, he was charged with examining and selecting the prisoners from the Auschwitz extermination camp.

The able-bodied—who could be used for slave labor—were sent to his right. The less able-bodied—who could be immediately gassed and cremated—were sent to his left.

114

115

In the previous image: Josef Mengele in Auschwitz selects those who will live and those who will die.

The photo was taken in 1944.

116

In Auschwitz, Josef Mengele conducted medical experiments that resulted in the disability or death of thousands of prisoners.

Educated at the Institute of Racial Hygiene in Frankfurt, he had a particular interest in hereditary anomalies, such as dwarfism, hermaphroditism and Down's syndrome. According to him, Judaism itself was a hereditary anomaly. In their natural state, all Jews were "monsters." And all "monsters" were Jews.

117

In one of his experiments, Josef Mengele selected two boys—one of whom was disabled—and cut them in half lengthways with a scalpel.

Then he sewed one child to the other: back to back, shoulder to shoulder, wrist to wrist—as if they were Siamese twins.

One of the boys was called Nino. The other boy was called Tito.

That's right: Tito.

118

Tito and Nino.

My sons are called Tito and Nico.

119

We are on Enseada beach in Bertioga.

On 7 February 1979, Josef Mengele waded into the sea on Enseada beach, had a brain hemorrhage and died.

I have come here with my sons Tito and Nico, on the trail of Josef Mengele. I want to wade into the sea in which he died. I want to dance on his corpse. I want to celebrate the value of the life of a disabled son.

I am the Simon Wiesenthal of cerebral palsy.

Josef Mengele is dead. Tito is alive.

120

On Enseada beach, I blow up some water wings.

Tito—the monster—wades into the sea. Nico goes with him.

Tito and Nico: one is sewn to the other.

121

122

In the previous image: my Siamese twins.

123

Tito improved rapidly at Padua Hospital.

On the second day of his life, he stopped having convulsions.

On the third day of his life, he could breathe without the help of machines.

On the fourth day of his life, he uttered a sound that the doctors interpreted as crying. On the fifth day of his life, he opened his eyes wide. On the sixth day of life, he took milk from the breast. On the seventh day of life, he was discharged from the neonatal intensive-care unit and placed in a room with my wife.

124

A week later, Tito came home.

125

We lived in the Palazzo Barbaro Wolkoff on the Grand Canal, next to the Palazzo Dario.

Who designed the Palazzo Dario?

That's right: Pietro Lombardo.

In the previous image: the Palazzo Barbaro Wolkoff, where we lived, and to its right the Palazzo Dario.

The painting is by Claude Monet. It dates from 1908.

I am at the window, cradling Tito and looking out over the Grand Canal.

Claude Monet stayed in Venice two and a half months.

When he painted my windows, his wife, Alice, wrote in a letter to her daughter Germaine:

*He's doing some marvellous work and, between
you and me, it's a welcome change from those old
water lilies.*

129

I am the Claude Monet of cerebral palsy. Tito is my water lily. He has become my sole subject matter. I devote myself entirely to him, he is my one passion. I never tire of my subject matter either. I always find in him an unexpected color, an unexplored shadow. Tito is the Absolute. Tito is Everything.

130

Pietro Lombardo designed the Palazzo Dario in 1486.

In the same year, Jacopo Sansovino was born.

Like Pietro Lombardo, Jacopo Sansovino is linked in circular fashion to Tito's birth. First, he designed one wing of the Scuola Grande di San Marco, completing Pietro Lombardo's work. Then he designed the Church of San Giuliano, adorning its doorway with a statue of Tommaso Rangone. Finally, he designed the Palazzo Corner, opposite the Palazzo Dario and the Palazzo Barbaro Wolkoff, on the other side of the Grand Canal.

I could see the Palazzo Dario and the Palazzo Corner from my window.

131

132

In the previous image: on the right, the Palazzo Dario, designed by Pietro Lombardo, and on the left the Palazzo Corner, designed by Jacopo Sansovino.

The painting is by Canaletto. It dates from 1738.

I am still at the same window, cradling Tito and looking out over the Grand Canal.

133

According to John Ruskin, the Palazzo Dario is an "exquisite example" of the domestic architecture of the time. The Palazzo Corner, on the other hand, built half a century later, in 1537, was "one of the worst and coldest buildings of the central Renaissance."

The Palazzo Dario expressed the soul of a true artist like Pietro Lombardo, who could also reason, but only occasionally, and who could even acquire knowledge, but only the knowledge he could pick up "without stooping, or reach without pains." The Palazzo Corner, on the other hand, expressed Jacopo Sansovino's academic pride, along with his geometrical fanaticism, which could "be taught to any schoolboy in a week."

The Palazzo Dario was "good for God's worship." The Palazzo Corner was "good for man's worship."

134

I never worshipped God. I never worshipped Man. However, I began to worship Tito. I began to worship domestic life. My gospel is an electricity bill. My temple is a greengrocer's shop.

Tito is Everything. A tomato is Everything.

135

The Palazzo Dario and the Palazzo Corner have spent five hundred years debating the great themes of humanity, shouting their arguments to each other across the Grand Canal.

If the Palazzo Dario was Socrates, the Palazzo Corner was Meletus. If the Palazzo Dario was Dante Alighieri, the Palazzo Corner was Farinata degli Uberti. If the Palazzo Dario was Don Quixote, the Palazzo Corner was Sancho Panza. If the Palazzo Dario was Naphta, the Palazzo Corner was Settembrini. If the Palazzo Dario was Lou Costello, the Palazzo Corner was Bud Abbott.

Only Venice could give me this.

136

After designing the Palazzo Corner, Jacopo Sansovino was commissioned to design the reading room of the Biblioteca Marciana — St. Mark's Library.

Pride of Science and Pride of State revealed themselves in his imposing vaulted ceiling in the Roman style.

In 1545, the ceiling collapsed.

That's right: *The Fall.*

Jacopo Sansovino was arrested and ordered to rebuild the reading room in the Biblioteca Marciana at his own expense. Jacopo Sansovino was forced to replace the imposing Roman-style vaulted ceiling with a flat ceiling.

I am the flat ceiling of cerebral palsy.

137

I moved to Venice in 1987. I was twenty-four years old.

For me, the best thing about Venice was its regressive nature. For me, the best thing about Venice was its nonconformist reactionaryism.

Living there was like living in an Amish town. I saw Venice as an Amish town for intellectuals. Its lofty irrationality is in sharp contrast to the enlightened popularism of my time. Its splendidly anachronistic nature makes a mockery of any kind of haughty progressivism.

A child from an Amish village who had not been allowed to be vaccinated could die of measles. In Venice, as I discovered some years later, a child could die at birth.

138

When I moved to Venice, I was writing my first novel.

After writing my first novel, I wrote my second novel. After writing my second novel, I wrote my third novel. After writing my third novel, I wrote my fourth novel.

When Tito was born, I was writing my fifth novel.

That was how I saw my future: living in Venice and jumping from novel to novel.

Tito's birth changed all that.

139

The first months of Tito's life were just like any other baby's.

He breastfed. He was taken for walks. He slept.

Every six weeks, we took him to the neurology department in Padua Hospital.

The doctors tested his reflexes and measured the size of his brain.

The results were always perfectly normal. The doctors assumed that Tito had escaped unharmed from his bungled birth.

140

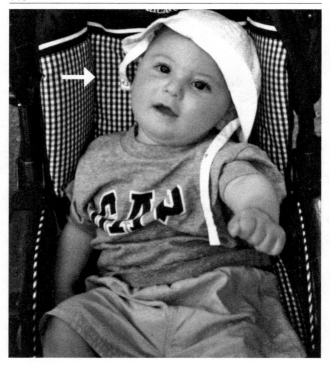

141

In the previous image: a perfectly normal Tito.

142

Just before he was six months old, Tito went for another examination at Padua Hospital.

His neurologist lay him face down on the stretcher. At that moment, he should have rolled over onto his back. Instead, he merely waved his little arms about, but—like a turtle—he was unable to turn over.

That was the first sign that he had cerebral palsy.

143

I had found out that my wife was pregnant exactly one year before.

I wrote about it on 23 February 2000 in my column in the magazine *Veja*.

I started by saying that, up until then, my rejection of fatherhood had been one of the rare, unquestioned certainties of my life. I went on to say that my wish—and I quote word for word—was to have "a turtle child, and whenever he became too agitated, I would just have to roll him onto his back and he would lie there, silently waving his little arms."

I got my turtle child.

144

Some days after the examination at Padua Hospital, we received the results through the post. According to the neurologist, Tito had suffered "damage to the extra-pyramidal system."

145

I know how to read.

Reading is my job. I think by reading. I feel by reading. When we received the result of the examination at Padua Hospital, I read all about the extrapyramidal system. Nothing I read prepared me for what we were about to discover.

146

Now I know what Tito has.

According to the neurologists who have examined him over the last few years, the damage to his thalamus was caused by his bungled birth. The thalamus is part of the extrapyramidal system. The damage is infini-tesimal, so much so that no machine has ever yet managed to detect it. But it's serious enough to affect all his movements.

Tito can't walk, pick things up or talk normally.

147

After examining Tito, the neurologist at Padua Hospital sent him to a physiotherapist at Venice Hospital.

During the weeks that followed, the physiotherapist put him through a series of tests.

It was only when all the tests were over that—with a feeling of fear and panic—I first heard the term which, from that moment on, would come to dominate my life.

Tito had cerebral palsy.

148

The fear lasted a week.

Then it passed.

The reason why it took only a week for the fear to pass was a fall.

Tito was sitting on my lap. I was sitting on the sofa in the living room reading the newspaper. My wife, who was rushing about, caught her foot on the rug and fell flat on her face in front of us. When Tito saw her fall, he laughed out loud. We both pretended to fall over. And he laughed and laughed and laughed. And we laughed with him.

Tito's cerebral palsy immediately became more familiar. Slapstick was a language we all understood.

Tito falls. My wife falls. I fall.

What unites us—what will always unite us—is the fall.

In the previous image: *Abbott and Costello Go to Mars.*

On a voyage into outer space, Lou Costello gets his astronaut's boot caught in a storm drain and falls over when he wrenches it free.

Francesca Martinez is a comedian.

She has cerebral palsy. All her performances revolve around that topic.

According to her, the term cerebral palsy can only have been invented to induce "fear and panic." That is why she likes to be described as a "wobbly" person. She is always wobbly, always about to fall.

Francesca Martinez's humor—like Lou Costello's —takes its inspiration from her falls.

Cerebral palsy is her astronaut boot caught in a storm drain.

152

Francesca Martinez told the *Daily Mail* what had happened to her.

Her cerebral palsy, like Tito's, was caused by a medical error. Her mother was left unattended for some hours because "being a Sunday there were fewer hospital staff on duty." Francesca remained in the womb and was left without oxygen for seven minutes.

Cerebral palsy, she explains, "occurs when part of the brain fails to work. It affects one child in five hundred. Each case is unique, but usually people's muscle control and mobility are affected."

The best way to describe how cerebral palsy affects her is that she appears to be "slightly drunk." Her speech is slurred and her balance wobbly.

153

Two weeks after learning that Tito had cerebral palsy, I wrote about it in my column in *Veja*:

My seven-month-old son has been diagnosed with cerebral palsy. From the outside, that piece of news might seem utterly desperate. From the inside, though, it's different. It was as if they had told me my son was Bulgarian. If I discovered that my son was Bulgarian, the first thing I would do would be to consult a book to find out more about Bulgaria: gross national product, principal rivers, mineral wealth, etc. And that is what I did with cerebral palsy.

154

After saying that cerebral palsy was a term that struck fear into the heart and that, for the first time in my life, I belonged to a minority, I ended the column in this shamelessly sentimental way:

I consider myself to be a humorous writer. For me, there is nothing funnier than frustrated expectations. Frustrated expectations about social progress. Frustrated expectations about scientific discoveries. Frustrated expectations about the power of love. I have always worked from that anti-enlightenment viewpoint. Now I've changed. I now believe in the power of love. Love for a little Bulgarian.

From that moment on, Tito's cerebral palsy became a recurrent theme in my columns.

Over a period of ten years, I devoted eight columns to him.

If, as Francesca Martinez estimated, cerebral palsy affects, on average, 1 child in 500, I published a column on the subject, on average, every 500 days.

Cerebral palsy affected the lives of my readers as often as it affects life in general.

In an article in the *Daily Telegraph*, Francesca Martinez stated: "That's the huge secret about disability—anyone with experience of it knows that a disabled person is just a person they love."

In my first article about Tito, that was the only "huge secret" I had to reveal.

Astonishingly, for me and for Anna, Tito's cerebral palsy was never a cause for sorrow. Astonishingly, for me and for Anna, Tito's cerebral palsy never seemed a burden.

At seven months, Tito was simply a person we loved.

In mid-2001, we took Tito to see a neurologist in New York.

In the previous image: Tito and me in New York.

In New York, I became Tito's first mode of transport.

He would point left and I would go left. He would point right and I would go right. He would point at his grandmother and I would hand him over to his grandmother.

Just like Josef Mengele, Tito would choose my fate by sending me off to the right or to the left.

161

The New York neurologist was very encouraging.

After doing a few tests, he predicted that, in two years' time, Tito would be speaking normally. He also predicted that, in four years' time, Tito would be walking on his own.

Both predictions proved false.

Tito never spoke normally. He never walked on his own.

162

Christy Brown had cerebral palsy.

During the first few months of his life, his parents took him to various neurologists in Dublin.

They all said that Christy Brown would remain forever in a state of "torpor," because he was an "idiot," "mentally defective," a "hopeless case" and "beyond cure."

In his autobiography, *My Left Foot*, Christy Brown described how he was able to overcome the worst prognoses, finding a way of typing and painting with the big toe of his left foot.

163

Like Christy Brown's parents, Anna and I learned to ignore all the doctors' stupid prognoses, whether positive or negative. Like Christy Brown's parents, Anna and I learned to celebrate each step taken by Tito, however wobbly.

After a certain point, we even learned to celebrate his falls. In the early years, Tito would always hurt himself when he fell. Over time, he developed new ways of breaking his falls.

Knowing how to fall is much more valuable than knowing how to walk.

164

The Irish band The Pogues recorded a song about Christy Brown.

In the opening chords, the electric guitar is accompanied by the sound of a typewriter, going *tap-tap-tap*.

165

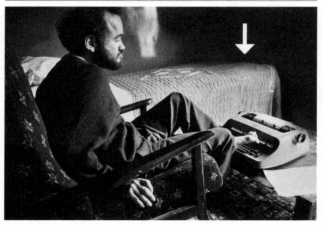

166

In the previous image: Christy Brown in his room, tap-tap-tapping away on his typewriter.

167

Now Tito is in his bedroom, and I'm in the library.

He is tap-tap-tapping away on his computer keyboard. I respond by tap-tap-tapping away on my computer keyboard.

I send him a PDF of a photo of Christy Brown. I then explain to him over VoIP that Christy Brown's cerebral palsy was far worse than his, but that didn't stop him becoming an important writer.

I also send him a file containing The Pogues' song and translate the words, which describe how Christy Brown, the village idiot, managed to become a respected writer around the world by typing — tap-tap-tapping — with his big toe.

Tito rapidly loses interest and switches off the VoIP.

Christy Brown felt a need to overcome his cerebral palsy. Tito is perfectly happy with the way he is. He doesn't need any good examples.

Christy Brown picked up a piece of chalk with the toes of his left foot and wrote the letter A. He was five years old. His parents realized that inside his paralyzed body was a normal mind, and they started stimulating him by talking to him all the time.

The New York neurologist recommended that we use the same method as Christy Brown's parents, because Tito's intellectual abilities were the best resource he had.

From that day on, Anna and I started bombarding Tito with words and more words. When he's had enough, he switches off the VoIP.

Christy Brown died when he was forty-nine, after choking on a pork chop.

To go back to Tommaso Rangone: the food that proved most harmful to Christy Brown's health was a pork chop.

Although the New York neurologist was wrong in his prognoses—just as the "idiot" Tommaso Rangone was wrong about Pope Julius III—he completely transformed our lives.

As well as recommending that we stimulate Tito all the time, he recommended that, during the Venetian winter, we go to live somewhere hot.

According to him, a child with cerebral palsy needed to be free and unimpeded and naked all the time. A child with cerebral palsy, according to him, needed to be in touch with the sand, the earth, the water.

171

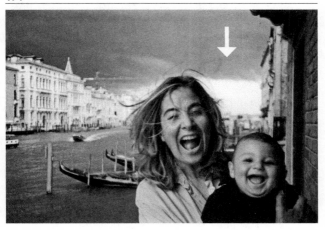

172

In the previous image: Tito and Anna witness the arrival of the Venetian winter.

I quote myself:

> *We each have our own particular talent. Mine is
> leaving Brazil. No one leaves Brazil as well as I do.
> If leaving Brazil were painting, I would be Rembrandt.
> If leaving Brazil were literature, I would be Shake-
> speare. From one moment to the next, I can abandon
> everything and leave. In a calm and orderly fashion. I
> have more than thirty years of practice. I have left Bra-
> zil at every possible opportunity and stayed away for
> long periods. And it's always worked out well. Because I
> know exactly what to expect of other places. Anyone
> who leaves thinking that he will find something better
> than Brazil is in for a disappointment. I never made
> that mistake. I left Brazil with the sole aim of being a
> long way from Brazil.*

When the New York neurologist recommended avoiding
Venice in the winter months, my first thought was to
buy tickets for Rio de Janeiro.

However often I had rejected Brazil, and I did reject
Brazil, I could never deny that it was hot.

Christmas 2001, we flew off to Rio de Janeiro.

It was hot.

Our plan was to stay for two months. We ended up staying for nine years.

176

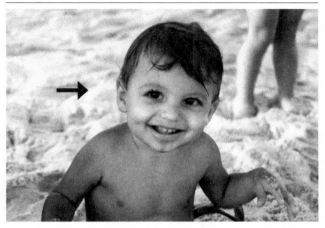

177

In the previous image: Tito on Ipanema beach.

178

I look back now at the photos from that time.

Tito is free. Tito is unimpeded. Tito is naked. Tito is in touch with the sand. Tito is in touch with the earth. Tito is in touch with the water.

In Rio de Janeiro, we found everything that the New York neurologist had recommended.

179

We stayed in Rio de Janeiro for nine years—instead of only two months—because of Ipanema beach.

There was another reason too: a Bobath therapist.

180

Karel Bobath was a pediatrician.

Berta Busse was a gymnastics instructor.

Born in Berlin, they had to flee Hitler's Germany because they were Jews.

Berta Busse arrived in London in 1938. Karel Bobath in 1939.

They married and together developed a physiotherapy program for the treatment of cerebral palsy, known as the Bobath Concept.

181

While Adolf Hitler, in Germany, was exterminating Jews and children with cerebral palsy, a pair of Jews who had escaped from Hitler's Germany were developing a treatment for children with cerebral palsy.

That's what Tito's story is like: circular.

182

Karel Bobath and Berta Busse both committed suicide on 19 January 1991.

He was eighty-five. She was eighty-three.

Together, Karel Bobath and Berta Busse developed a method for treating cerebral palsy and they remained together until the moment of their deaths.

Cerebral palsy unites people.

183

We took Tito to his Bobath therapist for one or two hours, four days a week.

He had his muscles stretched. He was tossed around in a net. He was put inside a cylinder and rolled around the room. He had an elastic belt tied around his hips. He had his legs immobilized and was then made to turn the top half of his body. He had adhesive tape applied around his lips to stop him dribbling. He was held in an erect posture in front of a mirror. He had to sit down with his knees straight. He was splayed across a large red ball and rolled backward and forward. He was thrown onto a foam mattress. He was encouraged to crawl.

My wife and I enthusiastically accompanied Tito's gymnastics.

We were happy in that place. We were as united as two old Jewish suicides.

185

In the previous image: Tito and his Bobath therapist.

186

Neil Young has two children with cerebral palsy.

That's right: two.

He is my guru.

187

Neil Young's first child, from his first marriage, is called Zeke. Neil Young's second child, from his second marriage, is called Ben.

Zeke was born in 1972. He has a mild case of cerebral palsy.

Ben was born in 1978. He has a severe case of cerebral palsy.

188

When Ben was two years old, Neil Young and his wife took him to the Institutes for the Achievement of Human Potential.

The Institutes for the Achievement of Human Potential persuaded them to devote all their time to Ben's treatment, giving him twelve hours of physiotherapy a day, seven days a week.

189

The Institutes for the Achievement of Human Potential is a sect.

If Neil Young is my guru, the guru of the Institutes for the Achievement of Human Potential is Glenn Doman.

According to Glenn Doman, a child with cerebral palsy needs to be continually manipulated by his parents, because if he keeps passively repeating a series of standardized movements over a long period of time, his brain will change and replace the damaged parts.

190

In 1981, Neil Young recorded a song about Ben's treatment using Glenn Doman's method.

It's "T-Bone" from the album *Re-ac-tor*.

It is the anthem of cerebral palsy.

191

In "T-Bone" Neil Young fanatically repeats the same two lines, for nine minutes and ten seconds, just as the physiotherapists at the Institutes for the Achievement of Human Potential told him to fanatically repeat Ben's movements, twelve hours a day, seven days a week.

In the first line, repeated twenty-five times, Neil Young says, "Got mashed potatoes." In the second line, repeated another twenty-five times, he says, "Ain't got no T-bone."

192

In 1989, some years after abandoning the Institutes for the Achievement of Human Potential, Neil Young, in an interview with the *Village Voice Rock and Roll Quarterly*, talked about Ben's treatment following Glenn Doman's method:

> *You manipulate the kid through a crawling pattern… He's crawling down the hallway, he's banging his head trying to crawl. But he can't crawl, and these people have told us that if he didn't make it, it was gonna be our fault… We lasted eighteen months. Eighteen months of not going out. Eighteen months of not doing anything.*

193

In the last thirty years, the Institutes for the Achievement of Human Potential, with its stupid Lamarckian belief that passive, repetitive movement can mold the characteristics of children with cerebral palsy, changing their brains, has lost almost all its followers.

It was all mashed potatoes and no T-bone steak.

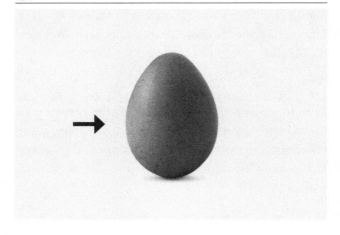

In the previous image: an egg.

Ben Young is now an egg producer. Instead of T-bone steaks, he has a farm in La Honda, with two hundred and fifty chickens.

During the treatment using Glenn Doman's method, Neil Young and his wife moved Ben for twelve hours a day, seven days a week. While they did this, Ben remained completely passive.

With us it was the opposite.

Tito moved freely about the large apartment in which we were staying in Rio de Janeiro, going from room to room, twelve hours a day, seven days a week. While he did this, my wife and I watched in passive amazement.

Tito was our Glenn Doman. He changed our brains.

197

How did Tito move?

He had a ride-on car made by Chicco.

At first, he could only move the car backward. In time, he learned how to move the car forward and sideways, pressing down with his two feet at once.

When Tito started to pick up speed and fall over sideways, we fitted the car with two horizontal bars to give him more stability. When he started to pick up even more speed and to fall forward, performing a somersault, we came up with the idea of screwing another wheel onto the front of the car.

Tito's falls had become as spectacular as Lou Costello's.

198

The greatest obstacle to a child with cerebral palsy is the impossibility of discovering the world around him.

With his Chicco car, Tito partially overcame that obstacle.

He would go into wardrobes and take the socks out of the drawers. He would go into the kitchen and tug at the cook's apron. He would pass underneath the ping-pong table while we were having a game. He would go into the bathroom and drag the roll of toilet paper around the whole apartment.

Tito was discovering the world. We were discovering Tito discovering the world.

199

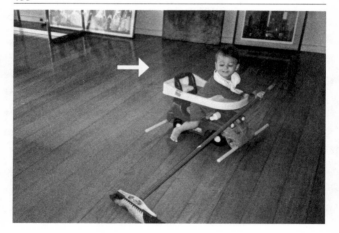

200

In the previous image: Tito in his car.

The toy car was Tito's second mode of transport.

201

As time passed, Tito's cerebral palsy became more and more obvious.

Other boys his age were running around and talking. He remained harnessed to the past, trying to crawl. His body was mutinying against his brain. His brain gave an order, his body disobeyed.

Tito was Dr. Strangelove, always trying to strangle himself.

202

At seven months, Tito was simply a person we loved. At eighteen months, he had already become a person with cerebral palsy whom we loved.

We loved Tito so much that we even loved cerebral palsy.

203

I quote from the column I published on 24 June 2002:

> *There is no more thrilling adventure than having a child with cerebral palsy. The worst enemy for a child with cerebral palsy is gravity. It's as if he were being permanently pursued by some crazed judo player who enjoys tripping him up. What he needs most of all is to learn how to fall. Then he'll leap from white belt to yellow belt, from yellow belt to red belt, until he reaches his limit. All the motor abilities that we acquire*

automatically, instinctively, he is trying to acquire through discipline, method, thought. It's the struggle of the intellect against savage nature. The perfect metaphor for the history of humanity. David and Goliath. Theseus and the Minotaur. Dr. Jekyll and Mr. Hyde.

204

205

In the previous image: one of the sixteen falls made by Lou Costello in *Abbott and Costello Meet Dr. Jekyll and Mr. Hyde.*

No one falls better than Lou Costello.

I ended that column published on 24 June 2002 in shamelessly sentimental fashion. I loved Tito. I loved cerebral palsy.

> *When people learn that my son has cerebral palsy, they look at him with a mixture of sympathy and pity. I look at him as if he were a totem: with devotion, reverence and a feeling of inferiority. They say that a child with cerebral palsy is better suited for living on the Moon, where there's no gravity. My son, therefore, is a man of the future, ready for interplanetary travel. You doubtless remember the* Star Trek *episode in which the aliens from a distant galaxy think that Captain Kirk is God? Well, I'm just like those aliens, and my son is Captain Kirk.*

Apart from saying that Tito was God, I also said that "a child with cerebral palsy is like Newton's apple: when he falls, he reveals the world's secret mechanisms."

Tito was my Law of Gravity. He was the principle by which I began to measure reality.

209

In the early years of his career as a neurologist, Sigmund Freud devoted himself to the study of cerebral palsy.

In 1897, he published his main work on the subject, entitled *Infantile Cerebral Paralysis*.

At the time, Sigmund Freud was entirely immersed in his research into neuroses. In one of his letters, he remarked:

> *I am working on a study of infantile paralysis,*
> *a subject that doesn't interest me in the least.*

210

Unlike Sigmund Freud, I was entirely immersed in my research into cerebral palsy, and neuroses didn't interest me in the least.

211

In the second half of 2003, we took Tito to a neurologist in Boston.

213

In the previous image: Tito in Boston.

214

We spent six weeks in Boston, in an apartment in Back Bay.

After examining Tito, the neurologist handed him over to his team of doctors.

215

The Boston doctors gave Tito a general anesthetic in order to inject Botox into his legs. The Botox proved useless. The Boston doctors gave Tito another general anaesthetic in order to give him an MRI scan. The MRI scan proved useless. The Boston doctors took a mold of Tito's legs in order to make him a pair of orthopedic leg calipers. The orthopedic leg calipers broke as soon as we got back to Rio, and they were thrown out. The Boston doctors made us order a walking frame. The walking frame wasn't right for Tito at all.

216

I spent thirty thousand dollars in Boston.

Tito's cerebral palsy cost me a lot of money.

217

Despite everything, I remember those six weeks in the apartment in Back Bay as a period of intense—almost irrational—happiness.

Because we were together. Because we were united. At that moment, I had the moral certainty of a fanatic. I had given up all my personal needs for something much bigger than myself. I worshipped Tito. Cerebral palsy was my sect.

The neurologist in Boston was useful in one respect.

He explained why, on his third birthday, Tito could still not say a single word.

He had dyspraxia.

The neurologist in Boston was useful in another respect as well.

He recommended that, in order to express himself, Tito should start using a digital communication device.

221

In the previous image: Tito and his Tech/Speak communication device.

222

The subject of "T-Bone" is Neil Young's obsessive attempt to give Ben some sort of mobility.

The subject of "Transformer Man," which is part of his next album, *Trans*, released in 1982, is Neil Young's obsessive attempt to communicate with Ben.

223

Neil Young used a vocoder to distort his voice on "Transformer Man."

He said:

> Trans *is the beginning of my search for communication with a severely handicapped non-oral person. "Transformer Man" is a song for my kid... People completely misunderstood* Trans... *Well*, fuck them... *You gotta realize—you can't understand the words on* Trans, *and I can't understand my son's words.*

224

"Transformer Man" is Neil Young's worst song.

It's deformed, unfinished, scarce half made up. It's disproportioned in every part. It's a foul bunch-backed toad. It's a bloody dog.

I find the very awfulness of "Transformer Man"
moving.

225

Neil Young's albums about Ben's cerebral palsy were the
biggest commercial flops of his career.

Cerebral palsy cost him a fortune.

226

In "Transformer Man," Neil Young offers a glimpse of
a robotized world in which a spastic child, incapable of
speech, can interact by using technology.

What his spasticity prevented him from doing alone,
he would, in the future, be able to do using machines
and by "pressing a button."

227

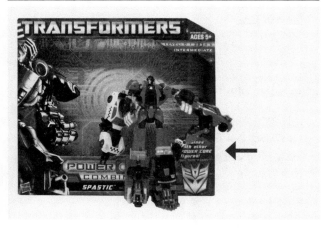

228

In the previous image: the Transformer toy made by Hasbro twenty-nine years after Neil Young released his song "Transformer Man" and sold under the name of "Spastic."

The future glimpsed by Neil Young was made real in the robotized world of the Power Core Combiners.

229

I wrote a column about Neil Young's "Transformer Man."

> *Neil Young had a collection of electric trains. Because his son Ben was incapable of making the trains run, Neil Young invented a gadget to help. The gadget was patented as the Big Red Button. With the Big Red Button, Ben was finally able to open gates, couple locomotives, make the train change track, let off steam and whistle.*

230

I ended the column by speaking again about Tito:

> *My son was never interested in electric trains, but he has a Big Red Button connected to me. He turns me on and off whenever he wants. He makes me change track, let off steam and whistle.*

Neil Young felt "electrified" by Ben.

I felt electrified by Tito. He was my "Transformer Man." By pressing the buttons of his communicator, he could finally talk to me.

In the previous image: the button Tito had to press on his communicator to signal a fall.

That's right: *The Fall.*

234

Tito's communicator was made up of thirty-two windows. Each window contained a symbol that corresponded to a word or phrase. When Tito pressed the symbol, the communicator would emit a recording of that word or phrase. Since the communicator had six channels, Tito had at his permanent disposal one hundred and ninety-two recorded messages.

235

The messages on Tito's communicator were recorded using my voice. He started speaking through me, distorting my words. Tito's communicator was my vocoder.

236

Tito's therapists were always adding new symbols to his communicator. He acquired a vocabulary of more than one thousand words, which accompanied him at all times.

When Tito was in a hurry, he would press the symbol of a rabbit. When he had diarrhea, he would press the symbol of a person sitting on the toilet. When he wanted to repeat something, he would press the symbol of two parallel arrows. When he was frightened, he would press the symbol of a green ghost. When he wanted to ask a question, he would press the symbol of a little

man with an egg-shaped face raising one finger. When he was annoyed, he would press the symbol of a little man with an egg-shaped face with steam coming out of his ears. When he was bored, he would press the symbol of the little man with an egg-shaped face leaning on one elbow.

237

Tito could communicate only through images, gestures, symbols, metaphors and analogies.

I had to interpret this. I had to adapt to his language. If he used images, I had to use images. If he used analogies, I had to use analogies.

That is how Tito became my God, my Law of Gravity, my Auschwitz survivor, my turtle, my water lily, my Lou Costello, my Richard III, my James Stewart, my Fall of the Bastille, my Jacopo Tintoretto, my Scuola Grande di San Marco.

238

Tito was the result of everything I had seen and read. In particular, he was the result of everything I loved.

239

At Christmas, in 2003, Tito was given a Kaye Walker.

In the previous image: the button Tito had to press on his communicator to ask for the walker.

242

Tito is now on his fourth Kaye Walker.

It's exactly the same model as the first, only larger.

Of all Tito's various modes of transport, the walker is the most valuable. He still uses it today to walk down the street. He will probably always have to use it.

243

Initially, Tito could take only one or two steps with the walker. He had to move in a straight line, because the wheels were locked in that position.

Around the middle of 2004, when Tito was getting better at controlling the walker, his therapist released the front wheels and I started walking with him in the underground garage of the building where we were living, in Avenida Vieira Souto, in Ipanema.

The garage was spacious and deserted. The floor was flat and smooth.

244

After exploring the garage, Tito became more confident and we set off to explore the garage of the building to the right. After exploring the garage of the building to the right, we went and explored the garage of the building to the left. Then, after exploring the garage of the building to the left, we explored the garages of dozens of other buildings in Avenida Vieira Souto.

245

Up until then, my sole talent had been my ability to leave Brazil; now, for the first time in my life, I was happy to be back in my native land.

The underground garages of Avenida Vieira Souto reconciled me to Brazil.

246

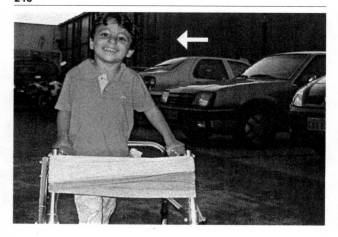

247

In the previous image: Tito in a garage with his walker.

248

Giacomo Leopardi was deformed.

He was four feet seven inches tall. Two large humps — caused by bone tuberculosis — made him a hunchback.

He was asthmatic and almost blind.

249

In one of his letters, Giacomo Leopardi said that his appearance was "wretched" and "utterly despicable." He also said that he had "only half of what other men had." He considered himself to be a "walking sepulchre" and expected death to come at any moment.

250

Just as I always wanted to leave Brazil, Giacomo Leopardi always wanted to leave Recanati, where he was born.

Recanati, according to him, was a "savage village," inhabited by "vile, vulgar people." He dreamed constantly of leaving "that filthy town, where the men were either asses or rogues—or both."

Giacomo Leopardi dreamed of leaving Recanati and never going back.

251

In 1822, Giacomo Leopardi finally found a way of leaving Recanati. He spent some time in Rome, staying in the house of an uncle. Contrary to the idealized picture of the city he had built up from reading the Latin poets, Rome seemed to him squalid and provincial, corrupt and full of prostitutes.

Giacomo Leopardi returned to Recanati six months later.

252

When he returned to Recanati, Giacomo Leopardi devoted himself to a life that was "entirely and solely interior." The fruit of that entirely and solely interior life were his *Operette morali* (Small Moral Works).

When I returned to Brazil, I too devoted myself to a life that was entirely and solely interior. My *Operette morali* were the underground garages in Avenida Vieira Souto. Tito and I would spend the day there, exploring their interior.

In his speculative garage, Giacomo Leopardi conversed with Torquato Tasso and with the Moon. Tito and I conversed with the porters of the buildings of Ipanema and with Toyota SUVs.

253

In Recanati, between 14 and 19 May 1824, Giacomo Leopardi wrote his "Dialogue between a Natural Philosopher and a Metaphysician," the tenth essay in his *Operette morali*.

The Natural Philosopher, inspired by the medical quackery of Tommaso Rangone, the author of *How Man Can Live for More than 120 Years*, reveals that he has discovered—"Eureka! Eureka!"—how to become immortal.

The Metaphysician replies that he is only interested in "the art of living little, because if life is unhappy—and it always is—the shorter the better."

Giacomo Leopardi's life was short.

He died when he was thirty-eight, after eating, in one night, a kilo and a half of cinnamon sweets from Sulmona.

To go back to Tommaso Rangone: the food that proved to be most harmful to Giacomo Leopardi's health were those *cannellino di Sulmona*.

In the previous image: Giacomo Leopardi dead.

For Giacomo Leopardi, unhappiness was man's natural state.

In "Dialogue Between a Natural Philosopher and a Metaphysician," he argues that "life and unhappiness can never be separated."

In "Dialogue Between Torquato Tasso and his Spirit," the Spirit sums up Giacomo Leopardi's Theory of Pleasure, explaining to Torquato Tasso that, since "the desire for pleasure is infinite, no real pleasure—which is, inevitably, finite—can ever satisfy that desire."

In "Dialogue Between Malambruno and Farfarello," Malambruno expresses the desire "to be happy at least for a moment." When the diabolical Farfarello tells him that this is impossible, Malambruno concludes that the only happiness available to man is death, because only someone who ceases to exist ceases to be unhappy.

Giacomo Leopardi, who was known in Recanati as "the hunchback of Montemorello," used disability and deformity as a metaphor for his "cosmic pessimism."

He wrote:

What is life? The journey of a sick and crippled man who carries the heaviest of burdens on his back and walks day and night, never resting, up and down steep mountains, through snow and ice, through rain and wind, and in the burning sun, until he reaches the edge of a precipice or a ditch and falls inevitably into it.

259

What was my life like in Rio de Janeiro?

It was the journey of a boy with cerebral palsy, who, with his walker, went up the ramps of the underground garages in Avenida Vieira Souto, which reeked of petrol and exhaust fumes, until he reached the edge of a step and managed to stop before he fell.

260

Happiness is Tito's natural state.

He infected me with his cosmic optimism. Devoting myself "entirely and solely" to him, I too was happy.

I had ceased to exist.

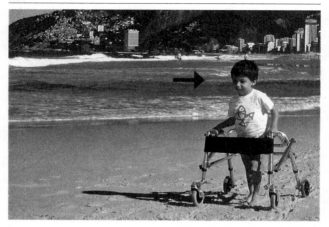

262

In the previous image: the little man with the egg-shaped face is happy—cosmically happy.

263

According to Giacomo Leopardi, happiness is always to be found in the past or the future—never in the present.

I was cosmically happy in 2004.

If I had to choose a moment in my past when I was even happier, however, I would choose the next year—2005.

264

Nico was born on 16 June 2005.

265

Nico's birth, in Rio de Janeiro, was the opposite of Tito's birth.

He was spared Dottoressa F. He was spared the amniotomy. He was spared cerebral palsy.

266

After experiencing a birth that was the opposite of Tito's, Nico became the opposite of Tito.

If one is behind, the other is ahead. If one is bent, the other is upright. If one falls, the other is always standing. If one is the comedian, the other is the straight man. If one is Lou Costello, the other is Bud Abbott.

Like Lou Costello, Tito is a baaaaad boy.

Nico is the opposite.

267

268

In the previous image: Tito meets Nico in the maternity ward.

It was the best act in our domestic vaudeville.

269

Karel Bobath and Berta Busse recommended that, during therapy, the child with cerebral palsy should look at himself in a mirror.

Nico was Tito's mirror. Tito was Nico's mirror. Nico could see his mirror image in Tito. Tito could see his mirror image in Nico.

270

Tito's cerebral-palsy world was Lewis Carroll's looking-glass world: time went backward, inanimate objects came alive, the laws of Nature were subverted.

In Tito's cerebral-palsy world, Nico played the part of Alice.

He was a "sensible" boy. He was exactly the same as other people — "two eyes...nose in the middle, mouth under."

Tito was exactly the opposite of other people.

He was the little man with the egg-shaped face from the communicator. He was Humpty Dumpty sitting on the wall. He was Humpty Dumpty losing his balance and falling off the wall.

271

Until Nico was born, Tito was practically mute.

His dyspraxia meant that he couldn't coordinate the movements of his vocal apparatus.

After Nico was born, he never stopped talking.

272

Tito's first words, like those of Humpty Dumpty, had "a temper, some of them — particularly verbs."

If Humpty Dumpty mastered the language of "Jabberwocky," the poem written in mirror-writing, Tito's language was Jabberwocky itself.

He reversed the order of the letters in a word. He reversed the order of the words in a sentence. He reversed the order of the sentences in a paragraph.

273

Over time, Tito's Jabberwocky became less impenetrable.

I could understand him. My wife could understand him. Nico could understand him.

274

In the latter part of 2005, Tito abandoned his communicator.

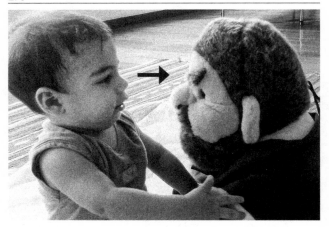

276

In the previous image: Nico examines President Lula.

277

For Christmas 2005, *Veja* asked me to write a column looking back over the year.

This was illustrated by Nico's photo, at six months old, examining Lula.

The caption:

In June, my younger son was born.

A passage from the article:

> I spent all year poking fun at Lula. I devoted more t
> han thirty articles to him. I promised to bring him
> down in 2005. I failed. Now I promise to bring him
> down in 2006. People said that my campaign against
> the President of the Republic was ideologically
> motivated. Not at all. I was only doing it for sport.
> Some people fish. Some people hunt. I just try to bring
> down Lula. He is my paca. He is my tapir.

Giacomo Leopardi described his own times as "stupid" and "dull."

My work as a journalist consisted in repeating week after week that my own times were stupid and dull.

Giacomo Leopardi called the inhabitants of his own town "asses" and "rogues."

My work as a journalist consisted in repeating week after week that the inhabitants of my own country were asses and rogues.

In the early years, I was able to reconcile my work as a journalist with my work as a father.

That changed after 2005.

I gradually lost interest in the asses and rogues of my country. All that remained was my interest in my home life.

The photo of Nico examining the President of the Republic was a way of declaring the supremacy of private life over public life.

Fatherhood became my ideology.

281

282

In the previous image: Tito picks Lula up by the ears.

283

In the same review of the year in which I published the photo of Nico examining Lula, I also published the photo of Tito picking Lula up by the ears.

The caption:

In September, my elder son managed to take sixteen steps.

If the most important event of 2005 was Nico's birth, then Tito's sixteen steps were the second most important event of the year.

284

I published a photo of Tito at Christmas 2005. David Cameron published a photo of Ivan at Christmas 2008.

Ivan was David Cameron's eldest child. Like Tito, he had cerebral palsy.

The decision to publish Ivan's photo became one of the big talking points of the electoral campaign in the UK. David Cameron was accused of exploiting his son's cerebral palsy.

285

David Cameron stopped being accused of making political capital out of Ivan's cerebral palsy only when Ivan died.

286

I exploited Tito's cerebral palsy and I continue to exploit it.

287

The reason I started exploiting Tito's cerebral palsy was the subject of one of my columns:

> *Montaigne was a devoted father. In one of his most famous essays, he wrote about paternal love and flaunted his daughter Léonor. Montaigne flaunted his daughter Léonor just as I flaunted my son Tito and Tom Cruise flaunted his daughter Suri. Léonor was the Suri of the Renaissance. In another of his most famous essays, Montaigne argued that to philosophize is to learn to die. I learned how to die with fatherhood. From the day Tito was born, I was completely cancelled out by him. I lost my will. I ceased to exist. Only a dead person can cease to exist. If philosophizing is learning to die, then fatherhood is the philosophy of the ordinary man, the philosophy of the poor in spirit, the philosophy of the masses.*

It is the only philosophy within the grasp of people
like Tom Cruise and me.

288

In 1635, Rumbertus was born, the first child of Rembrandt and his wife, Saskia. When he was less than two months old, he died.

In 1638, two and half years after Rumbertus's death, Rembrandt and Saskia had a daughter. Her name was Cornelia. She died before she was two weeks old.

In 1640, after the deaths of Rumbertus and Cornelia, Rembrandt and Saskia had another daughter. Like their previous daughter, her name was Cornelia. And like the previous Cornelia, she died prematurely, at two months.

In 1641, after the deaths of Rumbertus, the first Cornelia and the second Cornelia, Rembrandt and Saskia had another son. On their fourth and final attempt, it worked. The child survived.

The name of the surviving son: yes, Titus.

289

Rembrandt exploited his son Titus in the same way I exploited my son Tito.

He painted him reading. He painted him writing. He painted him holding a magnifying glass. He painted him with a sword and wearing armor.

When Titus was fourteen, Rembrandt painted him wearing a black beret and a pearl earring. When Titus was seventeen, Rembrandt painted him wearing a red beret and a gold chain. When Titus was nineteen, Rembrandt painted him wearing a black beret and a moustache. When Titus was twenty-two, Rembrandt painted him wearing a black beret and a fur coat.

290

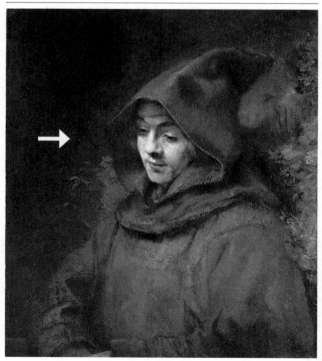

291

In the previous image: Rembrandt's son *Titus in Monk's Habit*.

The painting is by Rembrandt van Rijn. It dates from 1660.

292

Titus was Rembrandt's principal model.

Only Rembrandt himself posed for more paintings, with his seventy self-portraits — always looking through a looking glass, his image reversed.

As well as posing for portraits, Titus also posed, from his birth onward, for other paintings by his father, especially those that drew their inspiration from biblical passages. Rembrandt depicted him as Joseph, as Daniel and as the young Tobias.

In *The Evangelist Matthew and the Angel*, Titus is the angel whispering into the saint's ear. In *Christ Seated Disputing with the Doctors*, Titus is Jesus Christ. In *Christ Returning from the Temple with His Parents*, Titus is Jesus Christ. In *The Twelve-year-old Jesus in Front of the Scribes*, Titus is, again, Jesus Christ.

293

For Rembrandt, Titus was Everything.

294

If, as John Ruskin argued, the history of art can be divided into those who worship God and those who worship Man, then Rembrandt is the hero of those, like me, who only worship Tito/Titus.

295

John Ruskin wrote:

> *It is the aim of the best painters to paint the noblest things they can see by sunlight. It was the aim of Rembrandt to paint the foulest things he could see— by rushlight.*

According to John Ruskin, what marked Rembrandt out was the vividness of his darkness and the inexpressiveness of his light. The colors in his paintings were murky and fetid. Instead of illuminating beauty, he cloaked ugliness in shadows.

When Rembrandt painted the Virgin Mary ascending into heaven, he saw "only the lamplight upon the hair of a costermonger's ass." When he painted "an unsightly firework of unsightlier angels," he showed "the feet instead of the head, and the shame instead of the honour." When he made an etching of the parable of

the Good Samaritan, "we may see only in distance the back of the good Samaritan, and in nearness the back of the good Samaritan's dog," and the dog is defecating.

296

Tito was my Rembrandt.

His cerebral palsy obscured everything I had always worshipped. In particular, literature. What it illuminated—what became my sole focus—were the most ordinary, most domestic, most familiar aspects of life.

In that moment, I saw only Tito's deformed feet taking those sixteen steps. And in the foreground, I saw Nico defecating.

297

Rembrandt's finest work, according to John Ruskin, was his self-portrait as the Prodigal Son in the tavern, in which he is dressed as a gentleman, with his wife, Saskia, sitting on his knee.

Rembrandt is looking at us through the mirror, irreverently flaunting his private life and raising a glass of wine in a toast to domestic bliss.

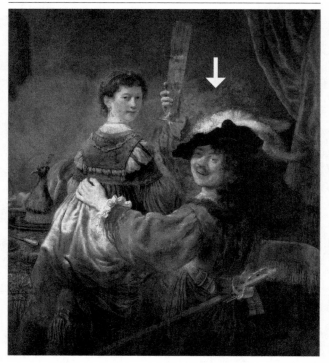

In the previous image: *The Prodigal Son in the Tavern*, also known as *Portrait of the Artist with his Wife Saskia*, by Rembrandt van Rijn.

The painting dates from 1635.

Rembrandt is the Prodigal Son. Saskia is the prostitute.

300

John Ruskin noted that in *The Prodigal Son in the Tavern*, Rembrandt could have portrayed the nobility of love and married life, because he was one of the greatest painters of all time.

But what did he do?

He again painted "the foulest thing by rushlight," illuminating "only corners and points of things, and those very corners and points ill and distortedly."

301

Man, for Rembrandt, is always imperfect and distorted —a falling body.

302

Like Rembrandt, I too was flaunting my private life and drinking a toast to domestic bliss.

My domestic bliss was represented by an imperfect, distorted boy, who, at that moment, was capable of taking sixteen steps without falling.

303

Marcel Proust in *Jean Santeuil*:

> *We had such a strong desire to understand John Ruskin's views on Rembrandt that, for this reason alone, we started studying English.*

What made me understand John Ruskin's views on Rembrandt was Tito's cerebral palsy.

Tito's cerebral palsy became my second language.

304

305

In the previous image: Marcel Proust by the Grand Canal in Venice, looking at my window.

306

Marcel Proust travelled to Venice in 1900, taking John Ruskin's books with him as his guide.

His walks through Venice and John Ruskin's books became the central themes of his own books.

307

We visited Venice every year.

In Rio de Janeiro, Tito used to walk with his therapist, but in Venice, in the holidays, he walked only with me.

He would go ahead of me, with his ungainly steps. I would be right behind him, ready to catch him if he should fall.

308

Marcel Proust remarked that a walk in Venice had the power to "educate the spirit," separating out the "intellectual aristocracy" from the "intellectual proletariat."

Throughout *In Search of Lost Time*, he refers constantly to analogies between the "aristocratic" memories of Venice and the "proletarian" memories of his characters.

The streets of Combray are mirrored in the streets of Venice. The face of Albert Bloch is mirrored in a portrait of Gentile Bellini. Albertine's dress is mirrored in a painting by Vittore Carpaccio. Domestic life in Aubervilliers is mirrored in a lost canal.

309

In the last volume of *In Search of Lost Time*, the Narrator stumbles and almost falls in the courtyard of the Guermantes mansion.

The incident reminds him of Venice's uneven paving stones.

Suddenly the events of his past life all fit together like a mosaic and he is filled with a sense of happiness.

He realizes that his memories of walking in Venice —along with the images and analogies they evoke —could give meaning to his life.

310

At that moment, the Narrator decides to write a book about his past life, because in order to interpret his feelings it is necessary, above all else, to transform them into ideas, to transform them into "equivalents of understanding."

The book he decides to write is *In Search of Lost Time*.

On our walks through Venice, Tito was always stumbling.

When this happened, I was filled with a sense of happiness. Preventing Tito from falling in Venice gave meaning to my life.

The book that transforms my feelings into their equivalents of understanding is this one.

314

In the previous image: Marcel Proust, dead.

The photo was taken by Man Ray. It dates from 1922.

315

In the weeks prior to his death, Marcel Proust ate just one croissant a day.

To go back to Tommaso Rangone: the food that proved to be most harmful to Marcel Proust's health was the croissant.

316

For Marcel Proust, a walk through Venice was the equivalent of reading Dante Alighieri's *Divine Comedy*.

317

In the *Divine Comedy*, Dante Alighieri is always counting the number of steps or paces from one place to the next:

There were less than a hundred paces between us.

Or:

We took ten steps to avoid the sand and the flames.

Or:

We walked a thousand steps along the solitary path.

Or:

We were separated by only three paces.

Or:

Even after we had gone a thousand steps, we were as yet as far from them as a good slingsman could throw a stone.

318

Walking with Tito in Venice, keeping right behind him so that I could steady him if he should fall, I counted each step he took, as if I were reciting Dante Alighieri:

Uno...Due...Tre...Quattro...Cinque...Sei...
Sette...Otto...Nove...Dieci...Undici...Dodici...
Tredici...Quattordici...Quindici...Sedici...

319

When Tito stumbled—and he always stumbled—I would stop him falling and start counting again from zero:

Uno...Due...Tre...Quattro...Cinque...Sei...
Sette...Otto...Nove...Dieci...Undici...Dodici...
Tredici...Quattordici...Quindici...Sedici...

321

In the previous image: Tito and I are preparing to ascend—in circular fashion—Dante Alighieri's Mount Purgatory.

The drawing is by Sandro Botticelli. It dates from 1480.

322

The sixteen steps Tito took on 28 September 2005 became, some months later, twenty-seven steps. Some months later, the twenty-seven steps became forty-four steps. Some months later, the forty-four steps became seventy-one steps. Some months later, the seventy-one steps became one hundred and eighteen steps.

Each step Tito took was complete in itself. Each step Tito took was a brief chapter of his story.

323

On 11 January 2008, Tito took three hundred and fifty-nine steps.

324

I commemorated this event in a column:

> *Edmund Hillary died on 11 January. On the same day, my son took three hundred and fifty-nine steps. Climbing Mount Everest, as Edmund Hillary did, might seem just slightly more significant than my son taking three hundred and fifty-nine steps, but for someone who has cerebral palsy, as he does, taking three hundred and fifty-nine consecutive steps without help, without falling, without smashing his teeth, is an epic event, at least in our family mythography. If my son is Edmund Hillary, then I must be his sherpa, Tenzing Norgay. He lurches from side to side, progressing slowly and uncertainly meter by meter, I remain in the rearguard, pointing out the smoothest route and saving him from falling. My son walked those three hundred and fifty-nine steps during the holidays in Venice. We are already planning our next challenges. First, we will walk three hundred and fifty-nine steps on Corcovado.*

Then, three hundred and fifty-nine steps in the Acropolis.
Then three hundred and fifty-nine steps along the
Great Wall of China. Then three hundred and fifty-nine
steps in the Sahara desert. Then three hundred and
fifty-nine steps on Mount Everest. My son and I will
travel round the world on foot, three hundred and fifty-
nine steps at a time.

325

Tito's steps became my unit of measurement. I began calculating all our journeys based on them.

In Venice during the holidays, the return trip to Bar da Gino took one thousand, one hundred and ninety-four steps. The trip from our house to Fondamenta delle Zattere, via Calle Querini, where Ezra Pound lived, was much shorter: five hundred and twenty-seven steps.

In Rio de Janeiro, the route from our apartment to Posto 9 on Ipanema beach was four hundred and eighty steps. The route from our apartment to the swimming pool at the Hotel Fasano was five hundred and seventy-one steps.

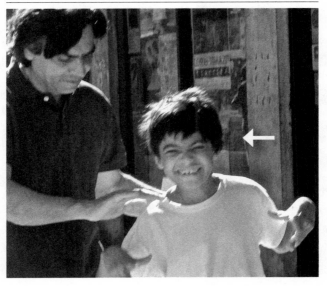

327

In the previous image: Tito and I are walking in Venice.
I am counting his steps, one by one.

328

A passage from my fourth and last novel.

The protagonist, Pimenta Bueno, who has injured
one foot and is unable to walk, is being carried on the
back of his servant, Azor:

PIMENTA BUENO: *Count the number of steps to Utiariti.*

AZOR: *One...two...three...*

PIMENTA BUENO: *I want to work out how far we are from our goal.*

AZOR: *...six...seven...eight...*

PIMENTA BUENO: *It can't be many more kilometers now.*

AZOR: *...ten...eleven...twelve...*

PIMENTA BUENO: *We've been walking for more than six hours.*

AZOR: *...fifteen...sixteen...seventeen...*

PIMENTA BUENO: *According to my road map, we should have arrived by now.*

AZOR: *...twenty...twenty-one...twenty-two...*

PIMENTA BUENO: *Never trust Brazilian maps.*

AZOR: *...twenty-four...twenty-five...twenty-six...*

PIMENTA BUENO: *We always get the measurements all wrong.*

AZOR: *...twenty-eight...twenty-nine...thirty...*

PIMENTA BUENO: *We lack mathematical reasoning.*

AZOR: *...thirty-two...thirty-three...thirty-four...*

PIMENTA BUENO: *We lack any real familiarity with numbers.*

AZOR: *Is it thirty-six or thirty-seven?*

PIMENTA BUENO: *What do you mean?*

AZOR: *I've lost count.*

PIMENTA BUENO: *You've lost count?*

AZOR: *I can't remember if I've taken thirty-six or thirty-seven steps.*

PIMENTA BUENO: *Start again.*

AZOR: *From zero?*

PIMENTA BUENO: *From zero.*

AZOR: *One...two...three...*

329

The novel was entitled *Against Brazil.*

It was published in 1998, two years before Tito was born and ten years before he took his three hundred and fifty-nine steps.

330

Counting Tito's steps in Venice, I could still reason, but only "occasionally," and I could even acquire knowledge, but only the knowledge I could pick up "without stooping, or reach without pains."

Counting the steps of Pimenta Bueno in Mato Grosso, though, I was only able to exhibit the kind of academic pride that could be "taught to any schoolboy in a week."

For Marcel Proust real life, the only fully lived life, was literature. For me, real life, the only fully lived life, became Tito. After his birth, I rejected literature and went off to earn some money.

To quote myself again:

> *Rimbaud beat up Verlaine. I envy Rimbaud. I would like to have beaten up Verlaine. I would like to have beaten up any symbolist poet. Verlaine took his revenge on Rimbaud some years later in a hotel room, firing two shots at him. I also envy Verlaine. He just wasn't a good enough marksman. In 1875, Rimbaud rejected literature and went off to earn some money. In only sixteen years, he did everything that anyone with an ounce of integrity would have wanted to do: he plunged into the Ethiopian desert; he bought and sold slaves; he trafficked guns of many calibres, thus facilitating the massacre of thousands of innocents; he got a tumor in his knee and had his leg amputated; he died alone in Marseille in terrible pain and praying to God, who, in his capricious way, refused to help him.*

When Tito walked three hundred and fifty-nine steps on 11 January 2008, I was earning money writing a weekly

column for the magazine *Veja*. I also earned money from *Veja Online*, writing a weekly comment column, and from *Manhattan Connection*, taking part in one TV program a week.

I became the Rimbaud of cerebral palsy. Journalism was my Ethiopia.

334

335

In the previous image: the propaganda from the Action T4 program, comparing the money the state spent each day on an invalid—5.50 reichsmarks—with the amount spent each day on a family of five—the same 5.50 reichsmarks.

336

Alfred Hoche was one of the inspirations behind the Action T4 program.

In 1920, in a small work entitled *Allowing the Destruction of Life Unworthy of Being Lived*, he calculated the financial burden of invalidity:

> *I estimate that the average annual expense of keeping an idiot alive to be one thousand three hundred marks. It doesn't take much intelligence to calculate the enormous burden this imposes on the national wealth for an entirely unproductive end.*

337

Twenty years later, these calculations were submitted to a detailed analysis by the economists of the Third Reich.

A chart preserved in the euthanasia center at Schloss Hartheim—that's right, under the command of Franz Stangl—calculated that the killing of 70,273 invalids by 1 September 1941 had saved the economy 245,955 reichsmarks and 50 reichspfennigs a day.

This was the equivalent, over a period of ten years, of 400,244,520 kilos of food, among which: 189,737,160 kilos of potatoes, 13,492,440 kilos of meat and sausages, 3,794,760 kilos of margarine, 531,240 kilos of bacon, 12,649,200 kilos of flour, 5,902,920 kilos of jam and, lastly, 33,731,040 eggs.

338

To go back to Tommaso Rangone: the food that proved
most harmful to the health of the people with cerebral
palsy who were killed under the Action T4 program was
the food they stopped eating.

339

In the case we brought against Venice Hospital, we had
—just like those Third Reich economists—to add up all
the money spent on Tito's cerebral palsy.

What with physiotherapy, occupational therapy,
speech therapy, equitherapy, a classroom assistant, an
orthopedic specialist, a neurologist, an anesthetist,
medical tests, Botox, a communicator, a walker, ortho-
pedic callipers, the hospital in New York, the hospital in
Boston, plus legal expenses, Tito cost, on average, 230
reais a day.

That is the equivalent, over ten years, of 3,497,916
eggs.

340

Because of the money they were taking from society,
the people with cerebral palsy who were killed under
the Action T4 program were called "bloodsuckers" or
"parasites."

My parasite was Tito.

According to Ezra Pound, the Jews were the real parasites draining money from society.

When he was sent a letter asking him to assist in protecting a German-Jewish pianist being hounded by the Nazis, he replied:

> *GET down to USURY / the cause WHY western man vomits out the jew periodically / the JEW won't take responsibility for civic order he WONT organize a state / he is a god damned Iriquois Indian / necessary defense against parasites / JEW parasite on principle / IF you are content to be sheep all right / but MAN declining to be GOY to jewish shearer will defend himself.*

I was content to be Tito's sheep. I was content to be sheared by my Jewish usurer.

343

Besides calling Jews "parasites," Ezra Pound also referred to them as "oily," "savage," "indolent," "filth," "worms," "lice," "cankers," "plagues," "snakes," "warts" and "syphilis."

344

In Canto XLV, published in 1936, Ezra Pound singled out the architecture of Pietro Lombardo as representing Good and usury as representing Evil:

Pietro Lombardo / Came not by usura

In the broadcasts he recorded between 1941 and 1943 for Radio Roma, he singled out Benito Mussolini as representing Good and the Jews as representing Evil.

For Ezra Pound, usury was a Jewish plot to enslave the world — "Jewsury." The "Hebraic monetary system," according to him, was "a most tremendous instrument of usury," and rather than a "war of the Jews against Europe," it was, in fact, a "war of usury against humanity." "When a nation dies," argued Ezra Pound, "Jews multiply like bacilli in carrion." That is why he recommended a purge of the Jews or a "pogrom UP AT THE top."

In the previous image: Ezra Pound walks along the Fondamenta delle Zattere in Venice.

On 6 August 2009, I went for a walk with Tito along the Fondamenta delle Zattere.

On that trip to Venice, I had decided to give up our old apartment in the Palazzo Barbaro Wolkoff.

In order to earn money for Tito—my Jewish usurer —I would have to stay in Rio de Janeiro forever, working as a journalist, and would never be able to come back and live permanently in Venice.

When we reached the Fondamenta delle Zattere, I received a phone call from my lawyer, Romolo Bugaro.

He said: "3,012,761 euros!"

Romolo Bugaro phoned me again a minute later to correct that figure: "3,162,761 euros!"

After seven years, the case brought against Venice Hospital had finally reached a conclusion.

Tito had been awarded 3,162,761 euros.

On the way back from Fondamenta delle Zattere, Tito and I passed Calle Querini, where Ezra Pound had lived.

My parasite had ceased to be a parasite.

Bimbo restò tetraplegico, risarcimento milionario

Tre milioni alla famiglia del piccolo nato in asfissia a Santi Giovanni e Paolo. Tardivo il trasferimento a Padova

Risarcimento milionario per un bambino rimasto tetraplegico, con grave ritardo psichico, a causa di problemi verificatisi durante il parto, avvenuto nove anni fa al reparto ostetricia-ginecologia dell'ospedale civile di Venezia.

La Ulss Veneziana è stata condannata a pagare oltre tre milioni di euro a titolo di danno patrimoniale e morale ai familiari del piccolo, una coppia di genitori veneziani, oltre a quasi 60 mila euro di spese legali.

La sentenza è stata emessa dal giudice Roberto Simone, del Tribunale civile di Venezia, a conclusione di una lunga causa, avviata nel marzo del 2004 dall'avvocato Romolo Bugaro, domiciliato dall'avvocato Stefano Gusmitta. Il parto finito sotto accusa risale al settembre del 2000: giunta alla quarantesima settimana di gravidanza, la futura mamma era stata ricoverata al reparto di ostetricia e ginecologia dell'ospedale di Venezia attorno alle 11 del mattino, con diagnosi di "rottura delle membrane". La gravidanza aveva avuto decorso regolare e la diagnosi prenatale aveva escluso qualsiasi anomalia cromosomica. Il personale dell'ospedale decise di procedere alla rottura artificiale delle membrane; attorno alle 12.35, si verificò una grave e persistente caduta del battito fetale e poco meno di un'ora più tardi i sanitari procedettero all'estrazione del feto, che era già in gravi condizioni a causa della

L'Ulss 12 è stata condannata
Il parto finito sotto accusa risale al settembre 2000

lunga asfissia, e ne disposero il trasferimento nel reparto di patologia neonatale di Padova con diagnosi di "sindrome asfittica perinatale", a seguito della quale è rimasto sofferente di "tetraparesi spastica da insulto anossico neonatale, associato con grave ritardo psichico e motorio, distrofia con microcefalia".

La Ulss 12, costituitasi a giudizio con l'avvocato Ferdinando Trivellato, nel corso della causa

ha cercato di dimostrare che le procedure adottate dai sanitari erano state corrette e che non vi era stato alcun errore.

Il giudice ha disposto una consulenza tecnica che, al contrario, ha concluso rilevando precise responsabilità da parte dell'ospedale in relazione «all'inadeguatezza dell'operato del personale». I sanitari avrebbero operato una manovra di "amnioressi" assolutamente controindicata e, successivamente, avrebbero ritardato l'estrazione del feto, esponendolo ad un lungo periodo di asfissia. «Appare evidente come la condotta del personale (...) si sia-discostato dal parametro della diligenza in senso oggettivo e da questa sia derivato un esito diverso da quello che ragionevolmente ci si sarebbe potuti attendere», si legge nella sentenza.

Il giudice ha quantificato il danno sia sul fronte del pregiudizio biologico permanente patito dal bambino, ovvero delle gravissime lesioni fisiche riportate, sia su quello del pregiudizio morale, e del lucro cessante, ovvero dell'incapacità di guadagnare per mantenersi, quantificando il risarcimento in circa un milione e 800 mila euro. Una ulteriore somma di un milione e 350 mila euro è stata riconosciuta ai genitori del piccolo a titolo di risarcimento per il danno patrimoniale e morale.

La sentenza potrà essere impugnata in appello, ma nel frattempo è provvisoriamente esecutiva.

Gianluca Amadori

In the previous image: the report in *Il Gazzetino* about Tito versus Venice Hospital.

Headline: "Child left quadriplegic receives millions in compensation."

353

Il Gazzetino reported that the civil court had ruled that the Hospital Santi Giovanni e Paolo should pay more than 3,000,000 euros in compensation to a child born in September 2000.

They also reported that the court had accepted all the arguments presented by the lawyer Romolo Bugaro, highlighting "improper conduct by the medical staff," "an entirely unnecessary amniotomy" and "a delay in removing the fetus."

354

Antonio, William Shakespeare's merchant, frees himself of his debt to Shylock, the Jewish moneylender, because he is represented in the Venice courts by Portia, a rich heiress disguised as a lawyer from Padua.

I freed myself from my debt to Tito because I was represented in the Venice courts by Romolo Bugaro, a novelist disguised as a lawyer from Padua.

355

During the first ten years of his life, Tito cost me 3,497,916 eggs.

From that day on, he began to produce his own eggs, like Neil Young's son on his farm.

356

In the last volume of *In Search of Lost Time*, the Narrator is filled with a sense of happiness because the memory of his walks over the uneven paving stones of Venice renders him "unalarmed by the vicissitudes of the future" and indifferent to "the word 'death.'"

On the walk back from the Fondamenta delle Zattere, after receiving Romolo Bugaro's phone call, I too was filled with a sense of happiness. From one moment to the next, Tito's future had ceased to depend upon me. I was free to die.

357

358

In the previous image: Ezra Pound's funeral in Venice.

359

In 1945, Ezra Pound was arrested and charged with treason for his radio broadcasts about Jewish parasites.

After twelve years in St. Elizabeth's Hospital in Washington, he was released and moved back to Venice, where he remained until his death.

I spent less time in Rio de Janeiro than Ezra Pound spent in St. Elizabeth's.

After only eight years, I began to think about going back to Venice and remaining there until my death.

360

Tito was fine in Rio de Janeiro. Nico was fine in Rio de Janeiro. Anna was fine in Rio de Janeiro. I was fine in Rio de Janeiro.

However, just as we always started counting from zero again whenever Tito stumbled and had to stop walking, Anna and I needed to go back to Venice and take up our lives where they had left off.

361

I'm looking now at the photos of our last months in Rio de Janeiro.

Tito celebrating his birthday in a barbecue restaurant. Nico playing football at the Flamengo football school. Tito with his walker, following a carnival troupe. Nico spotting a whale from the window of our apartment. Tito on his way to school on his tricycle. Nico watching the removal of a corpse from the trunk of a car.

We were fine in Rio de Janeiro. We were ready to leave.

362

363

In the previous image: Tito on his tricycle.

The tricycle was Tito's fourth mode of transport.

364

We disembarked in Venice on 4 August 2010.

365

Mark Twain disembarked in Venice on 20 July 1867.

He wrote:

> *What a funny old city this Queen of the Adriatic is!*
> *…If you want to go to church, to the theatre, or to*
> *the restaurant, you must call a gondola. It must be a*
> *paradise for cripples, for verily a man has no use for legs*
> *here.*

366

Venice was a paradise for my cripple.

For the first time, Tito could move around freely, by vaporetto.

Contrary to Mark Twain, he also used his legs.

Accompanied only by someone we hired to help him up and down the bridges, Tito went for daily four-hour walks with his walker, passing churches, theatres and restaurants.

According to Mark Twain, Venice by night seemed "crowned once more with the grandeur that was hers five hundred years ago." In the shadows, it was easy to imagine the city with its Desdemonas and its Shylocks, with its "plumed gallants and fair ladies," with its "noble fleets and victorious legions returning from the wars."

By day, though, Venice showed only signs of its fall from power. Mark Twain described it as "decayed, forlorn, poverty-stricken, and commerceless — forgotten and utterly insignificant." In the glare of day, the Queen of the Adriatic looked like "an overflowed Arkansas town."

Tito walked through Venice exactly as if he were walking through an overflowed Arkansas town, oblivious to Venice's glory or its fall from power. What mattered to him was being able to walk alone. Paradise was a place in which Tito could walk without my help.

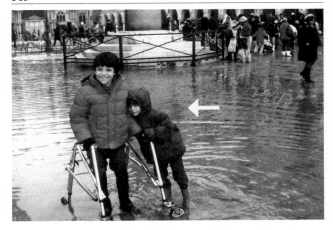

In the previous image: Tito and Nico during a flood in Venice.

Christopher Nolan had cerebral palsy.

He published his memoir, *Under the Eye of the Clock*, when he was only twenty-two years old.

When his book won a prize, he remarked: "You all must realize that history is now in the making. Crippled man has taken his place on the world's literary stage."

I was also working on a memoir about Tito.

My plan was to end the memoir with the story of an ascent of Mount Everest, which Tito would conquer three hundred and fifty-nine steps at a time.

My crippled man would take his place on the world's stage. History in the making.

Christopher Nolan was born mute.

During his early years, he could communicate only by looking up. When he did that, his parents knew that he was saying "Yes."

That's right: all he could say was "Yes."

When he was eleven, Christopher Nolan's father strapped a "unicorn stick" to his head.

From that moment on, Christopher Nolan began to communicate in writing, tapping with the stick on the keyboard of a typewriter.

376

In the previous image: Christopher Nolan and his father, Joseph Nolan.

377

In his memoir, Christopher Nolan described how the other boys at Mount Temple School in Dublin saw him.

They called him "weirdo," "eejit" and "mental defective." They wondered "if the cripple wore a nappy." They discussed his "lack of intelligence." They decided he shouldn't be in a normal school.

378

Christopher Nolan's isolation at Mount Temple School inspired R.E.M. to write a shamelessly sentimental song, asking: Why the other kids were always looking at him? Why did they laugh at him? What could he say? What could he do?

379

After seeing him every day, the boys at Mount Temple School eventually got used to Christopher Nolan.

It was the same with Tito.

The newsagent in Campo San Vio saw him every day. The old greengrocer saw him every day. The barber saw him every day. My wife's friend saw him every day. The man with the two dogs saw him every day.

The inhabitants of our overflowed Arkansas town got used to Tito.

380

My plan to conquer the world with Tito three hundred and fifty-nine steps at a time soon collapsed.

Now my one goal was to limit myself to a small area that went from the Ponte dell'Accademia to Campo della

Salute and was bounded by the Grand Canal and by the Fondamenta delle Zattere.

Tito had memorized all the uneven paving stones in our "town." His knowledge of those uneven paving stones kept him from falling. Instead of forging new paths, I wanted him to forge only old paths. Instead of entering unknown territory, I wanted him to enter only known territory.

My world now ended wherever Tito's steps ended.

381

As Gertrude Stein said of Ezra Pound: "[He] still lives in a village and his world is a kind of village," and the same was true of me.

382

383

In the previous image: Tito on the Fondamenta delle Zattere.

During the autumn and winter, he could walk to school on his own, using the Venice Marathon ramps, which the city council kept on the bridges especially for him.

384

At Mount Temple School, Christopher Nolan studied with members of U2.

They dedicated a song to him, entitled "Miracle Drug."

385

The song is a homage to the medicine that eased Christopher Nolan's spasticity, helping him to type with his head.

The name of the medicine: Lioresal.

386

In "Miracle Drug," U2 quote from the Gospel according to Matthew: "I was a stranger and you took me in."

The quote comes from the passage about the Final Judgement in which Jesus Christ, like Josef Mengele, sends off to the right those who deserve to be saved and to the left those who deserve to burn in everlasting fire.

According to U2, the scientists and doctors who developed Lioresal deserved to enter the Kingdom of Heaven.

387

Tito never took Lioresal. He never took any medicine. No one was capable of developing a medicine that would prove useful to him. Christopher Nolan's miracle drug was developed ninety years ago. People with cerebral palsy are still being treated with drugs developed ninety years ago.

388

389

In the previous image: *Abbott and Costello Meet Dr. Jekyll and Mr. Hyde.*

Lou Costello is transformed into a laboratory mouse.

390

Two years after Tito was born, scientists at the Medical College of Georgia placed stem cells in laboratory mice with induced cerebral-palsy symptoms and succeeded in achieving a partial improvement in their motor skills.

391

The results of the first experiments with laboratory mice led to stem cells being seen as a miracle cure.

In China, Russia, Costa Rica, in the Dominican Republic, in Turkey and in Cyprus, all kinds of medical centers sprang up, promising a cure for cerebral palsy with stem cells drawn from the skin, the spinal cord, from blood, from fat, from animal tissue, from placenta and from aborted fetuses.

According to a study carried out in 2008, the average cost of such treatments was $21,500.

392

Eleven years after Tito was born, an article published in the *Scientist* warned of the risks of "stem cell tourism."

According to the authors of the article, people with cerebral palsy who travelled to those medical centers in search of a miracle cure were exposing themselves to "unproven, and potentially harmful therapies."

The article described the doctors who offer stem-cell cures as "clinical charlatans" and "fraudulent."

393

Christopher Nolan's miracle drug was also fraudulent.

He died shortly before his forty-fourth birthday, with a sliver of salmon stuck in his throat.

To go back to Tommaso Rangone: the food that proved most harmful to Christopher Nolan's health was salmon.

394

395

In the previous image: Tommaso Rangone above the doorway of the church of San Giuliano.

The sculpture is by Jacopo Sansovino. It dates from 1554.

Tommaso Rangone is holding a sprig of guaiacum, the main ingredient in his miracle cure for syphilis.

396

In his memoir, Christopher Nolan frequently compares himself to James Joyce.

One wrote about cerebral palsy, the other about general paralysis caused by the syphilis bacterium.

397

James Joyce's Dublin, like Tommaso Rangone's Venice, was peopled by syphilitic sailors, syphilitic soldiers and syphilitic prostitutes.

In *Ulysses*, James Joyce used the morbid paralysis caused by the syphilis bacterium as a symbol of the intellectual and moral paralysis of his time. The episode in Bella Cohen's brothel—which he himself described as being written in "the rhythm of locomotor ataxia"—is the rhythm that best represents that paralyzed world.

Tito was my Bella Cohen's brothel.

398

The theme of *Ulysses* is paralysis. The theme of *Finnegans Wake* is the fall.

There is the fall of Humphrey Chimpden Earwicker — in Phoenix Park. There is the fall of Humpty Dumpty — the egg. There is the fall of Shaun — into the river. There is Shaun's other fall — also into the river. There is the fall of Finn MacCool — while skating. There is the fall of Eve — in the Garden of Eden. There is the fall of Issy and the fall of Troy.

No one falls better than James Joyce. Apart from Lou Costello.

399

There is another fall in *Finnegans Wake*: a drunken Tim Finnegan falls down the stairs and dies.

Then he comes back to life, like Tito.

400

In *Finnegans Wake*, James Joyce based himself on Giambattista Vico's theory, according to which, "History follows set phases, and the law that governs it is repeated eternally." For Giambattista Vico, humanity moves from the Age of Gods to the Age of Heroes, from the Age of Heroes to the Age of Men, from the Age of Men to the Age of Gods, and so on, endlessly repeating the same cycle of birth, progress, decline and resurrection.

That's what Giambattista Vico's *storia ideale eterna* is like: circular.

401

Now Tito and I are in Campo Santi Giovanni e Paolo.

I want to show him Venice Hospital. I want to return—in circular fashion—to the place of his birth. I want to relive his first fall.

402

Tito walks alone to Venice Hospital. I walk beside him, ready to catch him if he falls.

403

I count Tito's steps as if I were reciting Dante:

Uno...Due...Tre...Quattro...Cinque...Sei...
Sette...Otto...Nove...Dieci...Undici...Dodici...
Tredici...Quattordici...Quindici...Sedici...

404

Tito and I pass the statue of Bartolomeo Colleoni.

In *The Stones of Venice*, John Ruskin wrote:

I do not believe...that there is a more glorious work of sculpture existing in the world than that equestrian statue of Bartolomeo Colleone [sic].

In the previous image: the equestrian statue of Bartolomeo Colleoni by Andrea del Verrocchio.

The photograph was taken by Tito.

If Andrea del Verrocchio made the most glorious equestrian statue in the world, then I can say that I made the most glorious club-footed* boy in the world.

(* *The Portuguese term for clubfoot is* pé equino *or "horse foot."*)

* *The Portuguese term for clubfoot is* pé equino *or "horse foot."*

408

Tito continues to ride toward Venice Hospital:

> *…Duecentododici…duecentotredici…*
> *duecentoquattordici…duecentoquindici…*
> *duecentosedici…duecentodiciasette…*

409

After two hundred and eighteen steps, Tito stumbles and almost falls on the uneven paving stones in Campo Santi Giovanni e Paolo.

I catch him before he falls and start counting again from zero.

410

In his final poem, entitled "Wild Broom," Giacomo Leopardi describes an apple falling onto an ants' nest and destroying in an instant the results of the ants' vast labor, so painstakingly achieved.

I am Tito's ant. His falls are a constant reminder of the precarious, temporary nature of everything I have tried to build.

411

Now Tito and I are standing before the Scuola Grande di San Marco, the entrance to Venice Hospital.

I show him the finest sculpture on the façade, *The Healing of Anianus*, in which Mark the Evangelist is applying his miraculous cure to the cobbler Anianus's wound.

412

413

In the previous image: *The Healing of Anianus*.

The sculpture dates from 1488. It was made by Tullio Lombardo.

Tullio Lombardo was the son of Pietro Lombardo.

The photograph was taken by my son Tito.

414

Just as Pietro Lombardo created the Scuola Grande di San Marco with his son Tullio, I am writing this book with my son Tito.

This is all I can create.

415

Tito and I go up the disabled ramp and into the Scuola Grande di San Marco.

416

We pass the porter's lodge of Venice Hospital and cross the old atrium of the Scuola Grande di San Marco, now deserted.

417

Trecentocinquantaquattro…trecentocinquantacinque …trecentocinquantasei…trecentocinquantasette… trecentocinquantotto…trecentocinquantanove…

418

We reach the cloister where I saw Tito for the first time, in an incubator, with a tube up his nose and with his face green.

419

420

In the previous image: Tito in the Dominican cloister.

421

When I saw Tito in the incubator on the day he was born, I knew that I would always love and help him.

Since then, nothing has changed.

I will always love him. I will always help him.

422

In 1483, Pietro Lombardo and his son Tullio Lombardo were commissioned to produce a sculpture of Dante Alighieri for his tomb in Florence.

They portray Dante Alighieri in meditative mood, his hand cradling his chin, as he composes the *Divine Comedy*.

423

I continue to count Tito's steps as if I were reciting Dante Alighieri:

Quattrocentodiciotto...quattrocentodicianove...
quattrocentoventi...quattrocentoventuno...
quattrocentoventidue...quattrocentoventitre...

424

Four hundred and twenty-four steps.

This is the farthest that Tito has ever walked. As Dante Alighieri said in Canto III of his *Purgatory*, a good slingsman could still hit him with a stone. But as I stand, cradling my chin in my hand, it seems to me that a good slingsman could hit anyone with a stone, however far he walked.

Tito resumes his walk. I stop counting his steps.

Unless otherwise stated, images are from the author's personal archive. The images are listed here by chapter number.